THE FIRST AVIATORS

TIME LIFE ® BOOKS

Other Publications:

LIBRARY OF HEALTH
CLASSICS OF THE OLD WEST
THE GOOD COOK
THE SEAFARERS
THE ENCYCLOPEDIA OF COLLECTIBLES
THE GREAT CITIES
WORLD WAR II
HOME REPAIR AND IMPROVEMENT
THE WORLD'S WILD PLACES
THE TIME-LIFE LIBRARY OF BOATING
HUMAN BEHAVIOR
THE ART OF SEWING
THE OLD WEST
THE EMERGENCE OF MAN
THE AMERICAN WILDERNESS
THE TIME-LIFE ENCYCLOPEDIA OF GARDENING
LIFE LIBRARY OF PHOTOGRAPHY
THIS FABULOUS CENTURY
FOODS OF THE WORLD
TIME-LIFE LIBRARY OF AMERICA
TIME-LIFE LIBRARY OF ART
GREAT AGES OF MAN
LIFE SCIENCE LIBRARY
THE LIFE HISTORY OF THE UNITED STATES
TIME READING PROGRAM
LIFE NATURE LIBRARY
LIFE WORLD LIBRARY

FAMILY LIBRARY:
HOW THINGS WORK IN YOUR HOME
THE TIME-LIFE BOOK OF THE FAMILY CAR
THE TIME-LIFE FAMILY LEGAL GUIDE
THE TIME-LIFE BOOK OF FAMILY FINANCE

THE FIRST AVIATORS

by Curtis Prendergast

AND THE EDITORS OF TIME-LIFE BOOKS

TIME-LIFE BOOKS, ALEXANDRIA, VIRGINIA

Time-Life Books Inc.
is a wholly owned subsidiary of

TIME INCORPORATED

FOUNDER: Henry R. Luce 1898-1967

Editor-in-Chief: Henry Anatole Grunwald
President: J. Richard Munro
Chairman of the Board: Ralph P. Davidson
Executive Vice President: Clifford J. Grum
Chairman, Executive Committee: James R. Shepley
Editorial Director: Ralph Graves
Group Vice President, Books: Joan D. Manley
Vice Chairman: Arthur Temple

TIME-LIFE BOOKS INC.

MANAGING EDITOR: Jerry Korn
Executive Editor: David Maness
Assistant Managing Editors: Dale M. Brown (planning),
George Constable, Martin Mann, John Paul Porter
Art Director: Tom Suzuki
Chief of Research: David L. Harrison
Director of Photography: Robert G. Mason
Assistant Art Director: Arnold C. Holeywell
Assistant Chief of Research: Carolyn L. Sackett
Assistant Director of Photography: Dolores A. Littles

CHAIRMAN: John D. McSweeney
President: Carl G. Jaeger
Executive Vice Presidents: John Steven Maxwell,
David J. Walsh
Vice Presidents: George Artandi (comptroller);
Stephen L. Bair (legal counsel); Peter G. Barnes;
Nicholas Benton (public relations); John L. Canova;
Beatrice T. Dobie (personnel); Carol Flaumenhaft (consumer
affairs); James L. Mercer (Europe/South Pacific);
Herbert Sorkin (production); Paul R. Stewart (marketing)

THE EPIC OF FLIGHT

Editorial Staff for *The First Aviators*
Editor: Thomas H. Flaherty Jr.
Designer: Donald S. Komai
Chief Researcher: Pat S. Good
Picture Editor: Jane N. Coughran
Text Editor: Henry Woodhead
Staff Writers: Malachy Duffy, Thomas A. Lewis,
Sterling Seagrave
Researchers: Jane Edwin and Nancy Toff (principals),
Feroline Burrage, Marguerite Johnson, Clarissa Myrick,
Dominick A. Pisano
Assistant Designer: Van W. Carney
Editorial Assistant: Kathy Wicks
Art Assistant: Anne DuVivier

Editorial Production
Production Editor: Douglas B. Graham
Operations Manager: Gennaro C. Esposito,
Gordon E. Buck (assistant)
Assistant Production Editor: Feliciano Madrid
Quality Control: Robert L. Young (director), James J. Cox
(assistant), Daniel J. McSweeney, Michael G. Wight
(associates)
Art Coordinator: Anne B. Landry
Copy Staff: Susan B. Galloway (chief),
Elizabeth Graham, Cynthia Kleinfeld, Celia Beattie
Picture Department: Rebecca C. Christoffersen
Traffic: Kimberly K. Lewis

Correspondents: Elisabeth Kraemer (Bonn); Margot
Hapgood, Dorothy Bacon, Lesley Coleman (London); Susan
Jonas, Lucy T. Voulgaris (New York); Maria Vincenza Aloisi,
Josephine du Brusle (Paris); Ann Natanson (Rome). Valuable
assistance was provided by Nakanori Tashiro, Asia Editor,
Tokyo. The editors also wish to thank Martha Mader (Bonn);
Enid Farmer (Boston); Judy Aspinall, Karin B. Pearce
(London); Felix Rosenthal (Moscow); Carolyn T. Chubet,
Miriam Hsia, Christina Lieberman (New York); M. T.
Hirschkoff (Paris); Sara Day (Philadelphia); Mimi Murphy
(Rome); Janet Zich (San Francisco); Jo David (São Paulo);
Carol Barnard (Seattle).

THE AUTHOR
Curtis Prendergast has contributed to several
Time-Life Books series. After 25 years as a
Time-Life correspondent and bureau chief in
Paris, London, Tokyo and Johannesburg, he
now lives and writes on Maryland's Eastern
Shore. Research for *The First Aviators* took
him to familiar haunts in England and France.

THE CONSULTANT for The First Aviators
Tom D. Crouch is Curator of Aeronautics
at the National Air and Space Museum in
Washington, D.C. He holds a Ph.D. from
Ohio State University and is the author of
several books and numerous articles on the
history of aviation.

THE CONSULTANTS for The Epic of Flight
Melvin B. Zisfein, the principal consultant, is
Deputy Director of the National Air and
Space Museum, Washington. He received
degrees in aeronautical engineering from the
Massachusetts Institute of Technology and
has contributed to many scientific, techno-
logical and historical publications. He is an
Associate Fellow of the American Institute of
Aeronautics and Astronautics.

Charles Harvard Gibbs-Smith, Research Fellow at the Science Museum, London, and
a Keeper-Emeritus of the Victoria and Albert Museum, London, has written or edited
some 20 books and numerous articles on
aeronautical history. In 1978 he served as the
first Lindbergh Professor of Aerospace History at the National Air and Space Museum,
Smithsonian Institution, Washington.

Dr. Hidemasa Kimura, honorary professor at
Nippon University, Tokyo, is the author of
numerous books on the history of aviation
and is a widely known authority on aeronautical engineering and aircraft design. One
plane that he designed established a world
distance record in 1938.

For information about any Time-Life book, please write:
Reader Information
Time-Life Books
541 North Fairbanks Court
Chicago, Illinois 60611

Library of Congress Cataloguing in Publication Data
Prendergast, Curtis
    The first aviators.
    (Epic of flight)
    Bibliography: p.
    Includes index.
    1. Aeronautics—History. I. Time-Life Books.
II. Title. III. Series.
TL515.P68   629.13'09'041   79-25919
ISBN 0-8094-3264-1
ISBN 0-8094-3263-3 lib. bdg.
ISBN 0-8094-3262-5 retail ed.

CONTENTS

Lively images from a decade of progress

The year is 1904, the place a duned beach on the Channel coast of France. The man risking his neck in the experimental glider is Gabriel Voisin, who during the decade to come would graduate from gliders and become a prominent designer and builder of airplanes. The moment of his takeoff is captured here by the camera of a precocious nine-year-old boy, Jacques-Henri Lartigue, who would win renown in his own field, photography.

A few months earlier, on a strand much like this on the Atlantic coast of the United States, the Wright brothers had achieved powered flight. The age of aviation had begun, and France, having lost the race to be first, became the nation most determined to catch and surpass the Americans. Voisin and a cadre of others dedicated themselves to building a procession of newer and better flying machines.

Unlike the Wrights, who for years operated in the privacy of out-of-the-way places, France's first aviators performed their dramas of trial and error in public. They basked in the attention of their countrymen even when they failed. And their eventual successes stirred the national pride and imagination, causing people to turn their gaze upward (though not very high, as the planes generally rose only a few hundred feet, and sometimes much less).

Few were more fascinated by flight than young Lartigue, who strove to have his camera ready at the chugging sound of an approaching plane and in the process created his own record of the memorable first years of aviation. It was an era that was brought to a close all too soon, as the final photograph in this selection of Lartigue's work vividly reminds us, by the enlistment of the airplane—and those who flew it—in an all-consuming world war.

Gabriel Voisin sails off the top of a dune on April 3, 1904, at Merlimont, a French seaside resort where young Jacques Lartigue, who took this picture, was visiting with his family. Voisin's glider was based on one developed in the United States by Wilbur and Orville Wright.

A light Caudron biplane powered by a tiny engine takes off at Issy-les-Moulineaux, an Army parade ground near Paris, in 1909. Lartigue was 15 when he took this picture and, like many in his generation, was infected by the urge to fly. "In my sleep I fly all the time," he had written in his diary. "I cannot get enough of it!"

Auto, bicycle and pedestrian traffic stops to watch a biplane flown by Maurice Farman over the countryside near Paris in 1911.

A pilot scrambles to safety as his plane
crashes at Issy-les-Moulineaux in 1911;
a fragment of shattered propeller sails
through the air at top center.

French foot soldiers bound for the front in August of 1914 are overtaken by a Farman biplane. It was one of 138 planes in the burgeoning French air service at the beginning of World War I.

Rediscovering the secrets of Kitty Hawk

The age of aviation dawned not as a sunburst but as a tantalizing glimmer. Long after the Wright brothers had flown at Kitty Hawk in 1903, and even after they had gone on to perfect the first truly practical airplane, few people had heard of their achievement and fewer still understood or believed what they had done. The Wrights worked in relative obscurity and became obsessed with keeping the details of their invention secret. As a result, aspiring aviators elsewhere—particularly in France, where the pursuit of flight benefited from a robust aeronautical heritage—toiled to conquer gravity with an eclectic assortment of contraptions of their own design. Slowly and painfully they reinvented the airplane and, one by one, followed the Wright brothers into the sky.

The first aviators had only their wits and reflexes to bring them down safely again. Their planes, mere collages of wood, cloth and wire, were difficult to control and so sensitive to air currents that even moderate winds could knock them to the ground. The engines that pushed or pulled them were weak and unreliable, with a tendency to stop dead at crucial moments. Against such odds, the pilots risked their fortunes, their pride, their lives. Some died. For others the risks paid dividends of wealth and immortality.

Once flying was established, the fever infected people everywhere. Toward the end of the first decade of the 20th Century, the aviator emerged as an international hero, glamorized as a person apart from other mortals. The headlines of the world's newspapers proclaimed the exploits of this charismatic new breed of fliers as they competed for princely purses in the first air races and earned stupendous fees for exhibitions. Thus motivated, they pushed their planes to new limits of altitude, distance and speed.

Nowhere did aviation fever become more intense than in France. To be first to drive aloft in an "aerial automobile," as the new machine was often, but mistakenly, conceived to be, had seemed the birthright of the French. France was, after all, the country of the Montgolfier brothers, who in 1783 had first lifted humans off the earth by means of a gaily painted cotton balloon filled with heated air, and in 1884 French inventive genius had produced the world's first successful dirigible.

A Frenchman also claimed to have led the world in manned, powered (if not controlled) flight from level ground in a heavier-than-air machine. He was Clément Ader, an electrical engineer whose steam-powered,

France's pioneer aviators are celebrated in these postcards of the early 1900s featuring landmarks linked with their exploits. From the top: Ferdinand Ferber flying above the Champs Élysées, Alberto Santos-Dumont over the Arc de Triomphe, Léon Delagrange by the dome of St. Peter's, Count de Lambert at the Eiffel Tower, Louis Blériot crossing the English Channel, and Henry Farman above the cathedral at Rheims.

bat-winged *Éole* bounced briefly into the air in 1890. In 1897 Ader tried out another machine, named Avion III; it failed to fly but the word *"avion,"* for "airplane," became part of the French language.

A legacy so rich seemed to make manned flight in France a foregone conclusion, but strangely enough, French experimenters for several years ignored the signposts that might have led to success, focusing instead on balloon and dirigible flight as the most promising avenues of aerial progress.

There was one notable exception. Captain Ferdinand Ferber, an artillery commander and would-be aviator, almost singlehandedly kept the dream of heavier-than-air flight alive in France. Ferber's interest had been kindled first by the gliding experiments of Germany's Otto Lilienthal. Then, in 1901, he read a magazine article describing the experiments in America of another pioneer, Octave Chanute, the French-born civil engineer who was the Wrights' early counselor. By corresponding with Chanute, Ferber learned of the Wright brothers' experiments with gliders and began devouring accounts of their work in the scientific journals that Chanute passed along. Eventually the French Army officer struck up a correspondence with the American inventors themselves and developed a great respect for them. "Without this man," he subsequently said of Wilbur Wright, "I would be nothing, for I would not have dared to trust myself to a flimsy fabric if I had not known—from his accounts and from his photographs—that it would bear me."

Captain Ferber was one of those gadflies to whom the development of aviation historically has owed much. His own rather crudely constructed approximations of the Wright gliders lacked adequate control in flight and performed erratically. Ferber himself, moreover, was something of a military misfit; he slouched, sat a horse clumsily and refused to wear the glasses he needed for nearsightedness—as a result of which he once failed to salute the French Minister of War and missed promotion to major. But in his frequent lectures and writings on aviation—sometimes using a pen name, Monsieur de Rue, so that he could express himself more freely—Ferber exerted great influence on his European contemporaries.

One of Monsieur de Rue's most avid readers was a wealthy Paris attorney of Irish descent named Ernest Archdeacon, an ardent nationalist who would become the leading promoter of aviation in France. Archdeacon's dream, like Ferber's, was to see Frenchmen fly, and he put his considerable resources into making that dream a reality. An articulate man with a smooth manner, he had entree into every important circle. Aviation was not his only passion; he fancied locomotion of all sorts. He had raced cars, motorboats and balloons (once in a 75-mile-per-hour wind) and had even invested in a curious hand-and-foot-powered bicycle. In 1898, having seen Ader's Avion III, Archdeacon became convinced that mechanical flight was imminent; he began urging Frenchmen not to let the 20th Century arrive, as he said, "with-

The ardent patron of France's pioneer aviators, attorney Ernest Archdeacon was not himself a flier but he became a dominant voice in the Aero Club of France and was cosponsor of the world's first prize for achievement in aviation.

out having added this beautiful ornament to France's scientific crown." That year he helped to found the Aero Club of France, which soon became the nerve center of European aviation.

The Aero Club met in the elegant salons of the French Automobile Club, overlooking the Place de la Concorde, where a century earlier, during the Revolution, the guillotine had done its grisly work. From 1903 onward, the Aero Club itself became the scene of some agitation, as disquieting news about the American lead in heavier-than-air flight continued to reach and alarm Paris.

In April 1903, Octave Chanute came back briefly to his homeland (he had been in the United States since boyhood), and lectured in French to the Aero Club on the Wrights' advanced gliding experiments. His lecture, and articles that followed in French journals, virtually gave away the Wrights' essential secret—the ingenious system that enabled them to twist, or warp, the wing tips of their craft in flight. This wing-warping mechanism, for which the Wrights had applied for a patent, was patterned after the way a bird flexes the tips of its wings; it allowed the Wrights to increase or decrease the lift on one wing or the other, enabling them to produce a banking motion in turns and to maintain the lateral balance of their gliders, and later their powered Flyers.

Chanute's audience failed to grasp the essence of what the Wrights had accomplished, yet it was clear to everyone that the Wrights were far ahead of all other experimenters in the heavier-than-air race. Ferber sent a warning letter to Archdeacon, imploring him to rally immediate financial support for advanced gliding experimentation in France. "The airplane," he pleaded, "must not be allowed to reach successful development in America."

Then in December of 1903 came news of the Wrights' first powered flight, spurring a burst of activity within the Aero Club. Archdeacon commissioned a Wright-style glider for himself, to be built in France following the pattern Chanute had indicated in his articles. In March of 1904, Archdeacon put up 25,000 francs ($5,000) of his own money, matching an amount offered by the French oil magnate Henry Deutsch de la Meurthe, for a Grand Prix d'Aviation that would bear both their names. It would be awarded for the first officially recorded powered flight around a measured course one kilometer (.62 mile) long. The rules included a prudent stipulation: The airplane had to land intact.

The Deutsch-Archdeacon prize was still unclaimed when late in 1905 the members of the Aero Club received a stunning report from Ohio. In letters to Ferber and to the club secretary, Georges Besançon, the Wrights described their latest achievement: Over Huffman Prairie, a cow pasture near Dayton, their Flyer III had flown for 24$\frac{1}{5}$ miles, or 39 kilometers, landing only when its fuel ran out. The Wrights revealed no details of how their machine worked, and when the letter to Besançon was published in the paper L'Auto, the French were skeptical; some thought the American brothers must be outright liars. L'Auto immediately dispatched a correspondent to the United States to investigate.

From Dayton he cabled: "The Wright brothers refuse to show their machine, but I have interviewed the witnesses and it is impossible to doubt the success of their experiments." The emissary also brought back a copy of *The Dayton Daily News* that carried an article on the Wrights, which they had tried to suppress, and a crude sketch of the working details of their machine.

"*L'affaire Wright,*" as it was called, rocked the January 1906 meeting of the Aero Club. A shrill debate, it was reported, began after dinner, "at the delectable moment of the cigar," and raged on until midnight. Captain Ferber's supporters accepted the Wrights' claims, but Archdeacon refused to believe them. Let the Wrights come to France and prove themselves in public, he argued, and he soon issued a taunting letter to the brothers through the French press:

"I take the liberty of reminding you that there is, in France, a modest prize of 50,000 francs bearing the name 'Prix Deutsch-Archdeacon,' that will go to the first experimenter who flies an airplane in a closed circle, not of 39 kilometers but only of one kilometer. It will assuredly not tire you very much to make a brief visit to France simply to 'collect' this little prize."

Confident now of the market value of their invention, and unwilling to

At his estate near Paris in 1906, artillery Captain Ferdinand Ferber sits in the bizarre-looking "chariot automobile" that he designed to test the action of propellers. Ferber was the first person in France to grasp the significance of the Wright brothers' achievement, but his own initial attempts at powered flight were not successful.

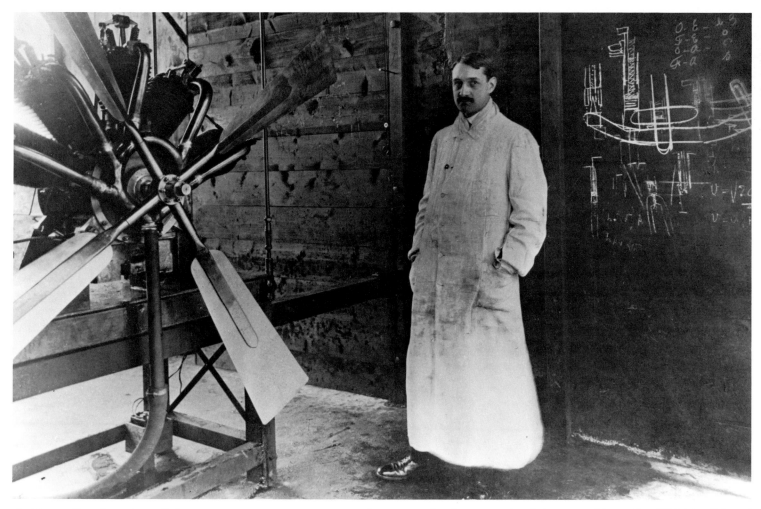

A visionary French engineer, Robert Esnault-Pelterie, shown here in his shop in about 1906, developed a successful air-cooled, fan-shaped engine that had seven cylinders. He also built and flew the first plane with an enclosed fuselage, which was constructed of welded steel tubing and covered with red muslin.

expose its secrets further to potential competitors, the Wrights did not even respond to the French challenge. In fact, they had stopped flying late in 1905 to devote their energies to selling their airplane to a national government, preferably their own.

Two more years were to pass before a European finally flew the circle and claimed Archdeacon's money. The failure of Continental aviators to capitalize on what was known of the Wright brothers' invention remains one of aviation's great enigmas—all the more so in that the French journal *L'Aérophile* published the Wright patent in January 1906, giving full details that had only been outlined in Chanute's earlier lecture and articles.

The failure may be attributable to the Europeans' rush to get into the air by driving "aerial automobiles" rather than to make progress slowly and methodically—"step by step, jump by jump, flight by flight," as Ferber had once prescribed. As it was, when Archdeacon's Wright-style glider failed to perform as expected—it was based on incomplete drawings—he abandoned it, rather than make the modifications that might have led to success. Another Frenchman, a young engineer named Robert Esnault-Pelterie, also built a Wright-style glider from sketchy data; when it flew poorly, he blamed the wing-warping system and substituted ailerons, or hinged surfaces, to maintain lateral control during flight. Lacking the Wrights' gliding experience, Esnault-Pelterie failed to recognize the need for rolling, or banking, in turns, and proceeded no further with ailerons. He did, however, publish his findings in a June 1905 article that spurred designers in several nations to begin experimenting with ailerons of their own. Eventually, of course, ailerons would compete with and then completely supplant the Wrights' innovative—but structurally self-limiting—system of wing-warping as the best means of lateral control.

No one better exemplified the impatient European approach to aviation than Louis Blériot, a prosperous manufacturer of automotive accessories who began to pursue flight shortly after the turn of the century. No pioneer aviator's career was more erratic; no early aircraft builder designed so haphazardly—often from mere thumb-and-forefinger indications, which he left to his shop crews to work out.

Blériot was an impulsive, reckless bear of a man, easily identified by his walrus mustache and prominent nose; he could be cold and mean, but just as often he exuded a magnetic charm. He was barely out of engineering school when, sensing opportunity in the burgeoning new automobile industry, he started marketing acetylene head lamps and such motoring gadgetry as foot warmers and luminous license plates. He soon coined a fortune, then proceeded to spend it on aviation.

Blériot was full of ideas; the wonder is that he survived them. Of the 13 different aircraft configurations he built or tested, more than half either failed to fly or crashed with Blériot on board. He was, moreover, a dreadful pilot. According to his contemporaries, he was uncoordinated, slow to master the basics and impatient with details. "As soon as we had fixed up a plane," Blériot's mechanic, Ferdinand Collin, recalled, "the boss, burning with eagerness to succeed, would try it out right away, without paying the slightest attention to air currents."

Once, while Blériot was testing a murderously overpowered tandem-winged machine, only his fast footwork aloft saved his life. "The monoplane took off like an arrow," he said later. "Very quickly I was up to 25 meters. I was quite impressed with this height when all at once the motor stopped dead. The machine started straight down. Figuring I was lost, I got the idea of leaving my seat and throwing myself back toward the tail. This maneuver almost succeeded; the plane leveled out, lost speed and rather slowly crumpled to the ground. I was not hurt." The craft, as usual, was a wreck.

In 1905, through the ubiquitous Captain Ferber, Blériot met Gabriel Voisin, a designer who was to become one of the great names in French aviation. At the time, Voisin was building gliders for Ernest Archdeacon, who had formed an "aviation syndicate" in an attempt to catch up with the Wrights. Voisin was also the syndicate's test pilot, and in that capacity he turned up one day on a bank of the Seine with the syndicate's latest glider.

The machine set the distinctive pattern for the aircraft Voisin would

Prophetic glimpses of aviation's future

The limitless possibilities of aviation are forecast in these decorative cards—from chocolate boxes of the early 1900s—which imagined the uses of flight a century in the future.

Fanciful as the scenes were, a surprising number of the developments they predicted soon became reality. Long before the year 2000, airmail had become commonplace, if not parceled out from mid-air as the card at lower left supposed. Flying squads of police pursued real-life criminals; air charters and air shuttles had become a routine way of travel for thousands. Fire was fought from the air and, at sea, people in trouble could look to the sky for rescue.

Some prophets were less prescient, predicting "men-birds" directing air traffic and pedestrians dodging empty fuel tins discarded from planes above. But others, like pioneer aviator Ferdinand Ferber, foresaw regular service back and forth across the English Channel and worried that "luxury and snobbishness will have commenced to invade flight." And author Rudyard Kipling, in a 1909 story, concocted what then seemed the unachievable—a transatlantic air route to link the Old World and the New.

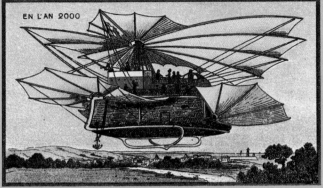

YEAR-2000 TECHNICIANS MAN AN AERIAL MESSAGE CENTER.

TENNIS PLAYERS USE FLIGHT PACKS TO GIVE THEIR GAME A LIFT.

BAT-WINGED POLICE CHASE AN AIRBORNE CROOK.

FIREMEN REACH NEW HEIGHTS TO RESCUE A MOTHER AND CHILD.

TRAFFIC CONGESTION IS RELIEVED BY AIR TAXIS.

A FLYING STREETCAR SHUTTLES FROM PARIS TO BORDEAUX.

A POSTMAN SAVES SHOE LEATHER WHILE GIVING PERSONAL SERVICE.

AIR RESCUE AT SEA DEPRIVES THE DEEP OF ITS VICTIMS.

later manufacture. To its boxlike main wings and tail unit, inspired by the man-carrying box kites of the 19th Century Australian experimenter Lawrence Hargrave, Voisin had added a forward elevator, clearly inspired by the Wrights. The test flight of this hybrid went without incident. Mounted on floats and towed behind a motorboat, it soared up over the poplars lining the riverbank and down again to a graceful landing. Blériot, who was watching, immediately ordered a somewhat different glider for himself.

Voisin agreed to build it, but he found Blériot's specifications alarming; the drastic curvature of the wing surface demanded by Blériot would rob the craft of its lateral stability, Voisin feared. He argued against it, but Blériot refused to listen. When it was ready for testing, Blériot's custom-made glider was hitched behind a motorboat and Voisin volunteered to take it up first. His concern over lateral stability was soon borne out.

"It was much lighter than my first glider and left the water almost without a run," Voisin reported later. "I began to swing from one side to the other. Finally my aircraft capsized to the left and went under water, taking me with it. I struggled in the tangle surrounding me, unable to see where I was. One of the piano wires had pierced my right wrist, another had gone into my left thigh and held me immobilized." Moments short of drowning, Voisin was hauled to safety.

Neither Voisin nor Blériot was daunted by this near-fatality. In fact, three days later they agreed to form a partnership to build powered flying machines. It was a union marred from the outset, however, by Blériot's bullheadedness. "My dear Voisin," he announced one morning, "for a week I have been making tests with models to discover the optimum shape for stability. I have come to the conclusion that a flying machine can only be formed of two cylinders of the same dimensions arranged in tandem."

Voisin recoiled at the prospect of this aerodynamic monstrosity. He managed to talk Blériot into flattening the cylinders into ellipses, but even so the apparatus failed its flight tests. A compromise configuration was adopted: Voisin's box-kite wings forward, Blériot's tail arrangement aft. On November 12, 1906, Blériot and Voisin carted their newest collaboration to the Bagatelle, a grassy field in the Bois de Boulogne, the principal park in Paris. The compromise machine only extended their unlucky streak: It came apart on the ground while taxiing.

Neither of the disappointed aviators left the Bagatelle early that afternoon, however. They joined a crowd of spectators and reporters who had gathered to watch a test flight by one of their contemporaries, the Brazilian-born Alberto Santos-Dumont. As it happened, they witnessed a milestone in aviation history.

The showmanship of Santos, France's adored adopted son, had made flight of various kinds a continuing spectacle for Parisians since the turn of the century. Santos had come to France in 1891, at the age of 18,

Missteps on the way to success, these ungainly craft were among the first designed by Louis Blériot, who finally built the most famous monoplane of its day. Above, the Blériot Model IV, with an elliptical tail, fails to fly at Lac d'Enghien in 1906. At left is the tail-first Model V canard, or duck, which hopped but did not fly in 1907.

rich with the profits of his family's coffee plantation. He was a dapper, elfin man, just over five feet tall and weighing 90 pounds, who wore collars three inches high, pin-striped suits and thick-soled American shoes to make himself look taller. He favored floppy white Panama hats and usually carried driving gloves. "I'm Santos, I weigh 41 kilos without my shoes but with my gloves," he would introduce himself. In his Champs Elysées apartment he ate at a table that towered 10 feet above the floor, the better to acclimate himself to airborne dining. Servants passed up the dishes from step stools.

An inspired gadgeteer (he is credited with conceiving the idea for the world's first wrist watch) and a talented mechanic, the young Brazilian began racing motorized tricycles, then turned to ballooning and subsequently to dirigibles. Santos and his primitive airships soon became the talk of the town. To the delight of the press, one morning he brought his dirigible down on the sidewalk beside the Champs Elysées and went upstairs to his apartment for coffee. Another time he dropped in on a children's party in the park and "kidnapped" a gleeful 7-year-old boy for a ride. For a Bastille Day parade, he floated overhead saluting the President of France with 21 shots from a revolver.

In 1904 Santos began to experiment with gliders. The next year he produced a helicopter with two large lifting screws made of silk-covered bamboo, and a third screw for propulsion. It did not fly, and Santos closeted himself again in his workshop.

What emerged in 1906 was one of the most outlandish-looking semisuccessful flying machines ever built. Dubbed a *canard,* in French, for its resemblance to a duck, Santos' monstrosity had a gawky box-kite rudder-and-elevator combination that projected far forward like the head and neck of a waterfowl in flight. From the cockpit the boxy wings slanted upward at a pronounced angle, like a bird's wings on the upstroke. A 24-horsepower engine driving a pusher propeller brought up the machine's stubby rear. In motion, it seemed to be going backward; even more awkwardly, the plane could be flown only with the pilot standing up.

Santos named the machine *14-bis*—"*14-encore*"—since it began its flying life suspended from the belly of his No. 14 dirigible. He intended that the parent dirigible lift the airplane into the air, where its control system could be tested.

Santos always drew a crowd, and reporters and spectators were out in force on the morning of July 23, 1906, as the *14-bis* was paraded to the Bagatelle for trials. According to one witness's recollection, Santos headed the zany procession in his Mercedes automobile. Dirigible and aircraft followed, towed by a donkey; a handcart loaded with 10 gasoline cans brought up the rear. At the park gates, a guard refused entry to the gasoline cart and asserted his authority by threatening to poke a lance through the dirigible; fortunately Ernest Archdeacon arrived and, once inside the park, had the gasoline from his car siphoned into the *14-bis.* Then, in a massive anticlimax, it was discovered that the plane

Brazilian-born Alberto Santos-Dumont, shown in the floppy-brimmed hat that was his trademark, was a Paris boulevardier driven by a passion to fly. "He acted," said one historian, "while others considered."

was in no condition to fly anyway—it had been damaged by bumping up against the dirigible. Calling for attention, Santos announced from the cockpit that the test was off.

Santos kept trying and on September 13, 1906, the *14-bis,* freed from the dirigible and given a more powerful engine, finally got airborne. It hopped for 23 to 43 feet (the estimate varying with the observer) and crash-landed on its tail. On October 23, Santos did better, keeping his machine aloft for seven seconds and covering about 197 feet. Excitement escalated with each advance. Captain Ferber, for one, hailed Santos as "the conquering hero" and predicted "a new world opening before man." Then, on November 12, with Blériot and Voisin watching from the sidelines, Santos made the longest powered flight yet recorded in Europe, covering 722 feet in $21^1/_5$ seconds.

The continent was electrified. At last, a European had taken off and flown convincingly. In London, Lord Northcliffe blasted the editors of his *Daily Mail* for underplaying the story. "Santos-Dumont flies 722 feet!" he shouted into the telephone. "Let me tell you, there will be no more sleeping safely behind the wooden walls of old England with the Channel as our safety moat. If war comes," he warned, "the aerial chariots of the enemy will descend on British soil."

Amid such hysteria, Octave Chanute wrote to the Wright brothers, giving a calmer appraisal of Santos-Dumont's achievement. "I fancy he is now very nearly where you were in 1904," he remarked dryly. In fact, Chanute was overstating the case. France—and the rest of Europe— lagged even further than that behind the Wrights. In England, an expatriate American named Samuel Franklin Cody, who had successfully flown a man-carrying kite, was working on a design for a flying machine. But it would be 1908 before he had it built and made the first sustained flight recorded in Britain. In Denmark, an engineer named J. C. H. Ellehammer had built a monoplane with a sail and in 1906 had flown it—at the end of a tether. That same year, the Rumanian Trajan Vuia managed some five takeoffs in a monoplane but failed to stay aloft for more than three seconds at a time.

However modest their gains, the Europeans at least were making their attempts at flight publicly, often before large and appreciative crowds. They garnered headlines and praise that eluded the Wright brothers, who had grounded themselves to devote full time to negotiating the sale of their invention. Nevertheless, the Wrights confidently felt that they were in a seller's market. "When we see men laboring year after year on points we overcame in a few weeks," Wilbur wrote bullishly to Chanute in October 1906, "we do not believe there is one chance in a hundred that anyone will have a machine of the least practical usefulness within five years."

But the Wrights' offer to supply a working airplane had so far piqued little interest among the governments of the world. American officials in 1905 had told the Wrights the nation had "no requirements" for a flying machine. British and French military leaders were somewhat more re-

Santos-Dumont tests the controls of his first plane, 14-bis, by suspending it under his No. 14 airship during the summer of 1906.

On its own, the 14-bis takes off in the Bois de Boulogne on October 23, 1906, for the first successful powered flight in Europe.

ceptive, but the Wrights' asking price of $200,000 seemed high to them, and the brothers' almost paranoid secretiveness about their invention made them exasperating to deal with. Even after the patents they had applied for were granted, beginning in July of 1904, they refused to reveal details of their machine, much less the machine itself, to prospective buyers in advance of a firm agreement. And as the Wrights concentrated on business, the memory of their achievements at Kitty Hawk and Huffman Prairie grew progressively dimmer.

Two years had passed since the Wrights' last flight in Ohio—and 14 months since Santos-Dumont's brief hops in Paris—when Henry Farman, a young man of Anglo-French heritage, accomplished a feat that seemed to establish European ascendency in aviation.

Farman was an aviator in the gentleman-sportsman tradition, the son of an affluent English newspaper correspondent based in Paris. Henry, or Henri (he used the English and French spellings of his name indiscriminately) had studied painting at Paris' famous École des Beaux Arts. While there he had become fascinated with racing, first bicycles and subsequently motorcycles and automobiles.

A small, handsome man with a closely cropped brown beard, Farman sounded like a Frenchman even when he spoke in English, but his style was unflappably British. A skid on a mountain road during an automobile race once sent him and his mechanic spinning into the trees; there, hanging from a branch, Farman coolly reached for a cigarette and called to the mechanic, who was dangling from another branch: "Pass me a match, Jules."

Opting in 1907 for what he called the "safer" sport of flying, Farman walked unannounced one day into the small Voisin plant in Paris and ordered one of the new models that Gabriel Voisin, having broken with Blériot, was now building with his brother, Charles.

Farman had set himself a goal—to win the Deutsch-Archdeacon prize. Other hopeful aviators, some serious and some merely whimsical, had the same idea, and business at Voisin Frères was booming. Each customer, according to Gabriel Voisin, seemed to have his own idea of what a proper plane should be, ordering "remarkable and unexpected structures, all more or less wild."

One client, a Russian prince, ordered a plane with the propeller built in the shape of a spiral staircase. A Dutchman wanted wings attached "onto a kind of car," with a tail sticking out behind. When this oddity was tested, the tail lifted as the propeller whirled, but everything else remained earthbound. Even those clients who ordered standard Voisin models wanted their machines personalized, a problem that Charles Voisin solved by painting the name of the customer on his plane's tail in large letters, overshadowing the smaller name of the manufacturer.

The early Voisin was little more than an enormous box kite, with an elevator in front, an engine with a rather crude metal propeller, and a rudder in a large biplane tail. Although the Voisins boasted that their standard model was easy to fly, at least one pioneer pilot remembered otherwise. "One could just force it through the air," he said. The plane had no side control, the same critic recalled, "so if you tilted one side down you had to turn the rudder to force yourself back again onto a level keel. It was quite a tricky maneuver."

Whatever the defects of the frail Voisin craft, Henry Farman was not long in overcoming them. He was, as Gabriel Voisin said, "manipulative skill personified." A few weeks after taking delivery on his plane, Farman was flying. He also began to make changes in the plane's design (soon, as it turned out, he would go into aircraft manufacture himself). He adjusted the trim, installed a Wright-style front rudder, and cut down the tail area to save 70 pounds in weight and reduce drag. It was in this modified Voisin that Farman, on January 13, 1908, made his bid for the 50,000-franc prize.

"Gliding upwards to a height of four meters, it crosses the line between the posts, with a flying start," the magazine American Aeronaut reported in play-by-play fashion of Farman's flight. "Straight and true as an arrow it makes for the turning point 500 meters distant, rising meantime by an adroit maneuver of the 'equilibrizer' to about 12 meters and remaining at that altitude. It rounds the far post 100 meters away from the path of its graceful curve.

"The great bird is coming back," the magazine report continued, "gradually sinking to four meters until after recrossing the line, when the apparatus is let down softly to the ground."

Farman had won the prize. It had taken him one minute and 28 seconds to complete Europe's, and the world's, first officially recorded one-kilometer circuit. It was an achievement the Wrights, unofficially, had far surpassed more than two years earlier. Moreover, Farman had made a wide, almost flat turn as he yawed clumsily around the course. His airplane was incapable of the tight, steeply banked turns made easily by the Wright Flyers, with their wing-warping device. But such aerodynamic subtleties were lost, both on the public and on the aviators present. The Wrights were all but forgotten; Henry Farman was the man of the hour.

He was mobbed, feted, hailed in editorial paroxysms. Even the staid Times of London uncorseted itself: "Today has been an epoch-making date, that of the victory before official witnesses of human intelligence in its efforts to solve the problem which brought Icarus to grief, which tormented the brain of Leonardo da Vinci. Nothing of the kind has ever been accomplished before."

Farman allowed himself to be caught up in the common euphoria. Four months later, with more flying time logged, he challenged the Wrights to a fly-off for cash stakes: $5,000 for a speed-and-distance contest, to be held in France.

The challenge reached the Wrights at Kitty Hawk, where they had recently resumed flying after two years of trying to market their invention. The sales effort was finally beginning to pay off. In February 1908

Society patrons of French aviation, among them the Baroness de Laroche and industrialist Henry Deutsch de la Meurthe (talking at far right), visit the Voisin factory at Billancourt in this 1908 painting. Gabriel Voisin is at center, leaning on the plane.

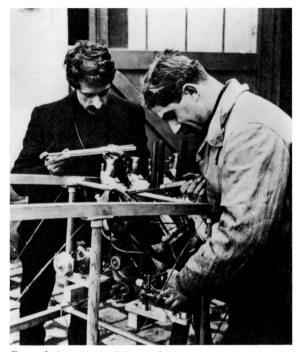

France's first successful aircraft manufacturers, Gabriel (left) and Charles Voisin, work on an engine in 1907.

they had reached agreement with the United States War Department on a price of $25,000 for a machine that they were sure was far ahead of anything else in the world. With an improved 30-horsepower engine pushing it along at 40 miles per hour, the Wrights' new Flyer, which is often referred to today as the Model A, was a marked advance over their earlier planes. It had upright seating for two persons and dual controls for instruction.

The Wrights had decided to divide their forces for a time. Orville would take charge of demonstrating the new machine for the United States Army at Fort Myer, Virginia. Wilbur would sail for France. Earlier discussions with the French government had broken down and a Model A the Wrights had hopefully shipped to France in 1907 was still locked in the customs warehouse at Le Havre. However, a syndicate of French businessmen had agreed to manufacture the Wright machines, on license, provided that one of the brothers would successfully demonstrate the airplane in France.

Wilbur was getting ready to leave America when newspapermen confronted him with the challenge from Farman. Well, would he race the European champion or not? "Mr. Wright smiled and said there would be no answer to the question," reported *The New York Times*. "He would not comment on the challenge in any way." It was a typical

Cheered to the finish on January 13, 1908, Anglo-French flier Henry Farman wins the 50,000-franc Grand Prix d'Aviation and the coveted Archdeacon

Wright response. Wilbur had little use for verbosity and he decried what he called the circus aspects of flying, a category in which he placed Farman's challenge. One day soon he would be flying in France, with his French detractors looking on, and he was confident that no words would be necessary then.

Initially, Wilbur Wright's reception in France in June 1908 was depressing. Customs officials had smashed his plane while inspecting the crates it came in—Wilbur mistakenly blamed Orville for a bad packing job, saying he could have done better himself with a scoop shovel—and weeks of work would be needed to repair and assemble it. But Wilbur was pleased to learn that the Wrights' potential French customers had found him a good, inexpensive exhibition ground at the Hunaudières race track near Le Mans, some 115 miles southwest of Paris.

In one corner of a Le Mans automobile factory owned by the president of the regional Aero Club, Wilbur began reassembling the battered parts of his airplane. The local workmen he hired spoke no English, and Wilbur spoke only an Ohio approximation of French. But he kept the

Cup for Europe's first flight over a one-kilometer circuit. Two years earlier, the Wright brothers had flown 39 times that distance near Dayton, Ohio.

same hours as his men and knocked off promptly for lunch, and they got on well together. For six weeks, as work on the Flyer progressed, skepticism mounted in the French press. The flying news elsewhere was more titillating, in any case. A fashionable Parisian sculptor, Léon Delagrange, had taken up aviation, and in Turin, Italy, he had given his pretty pupil, Thérèse Peltier, a ride in his Voisin. Mademoiselle Peltier thus became the first woman ever to go up in a plane.

At Le Mans, Wilbur's relations with the French press were not improved by nasty brushes he had with photographers who tried to snap "unauthorized" pictures in violation of an exclusive deal he naïvely had made with a New York magazine. Finally, Wilbur decided that although the Flyer was not quite ready, "it would be a good thing to do a little something."

Word of Wilbur's decision spread, and on Saturday morning, August 8, a crowd began to gather at the race track. It included Blériot, Archdeacon, leading French aviation writer François Peyrey, two officers from the Russian embassy in Paris, and many others—by far the largest and most knowledgeable audience yet to observe a Wright flight.

It was late afternoon before the rail the Wrights used for takeoff was laid and its pulley-operated launching derrick set. Wilbur, wearing a gray business suit, gray cap and his usual starched collar, climbed into the machine, which, like all the Wrights' previous designs, was equipped with skids rather than wheels. Once the engine sputtered and died; Wilbur's back collar stud had become caught on the control wires. Finally the weight in the launching derrick dropped, and the Flyer whooshed into the air.

"We beheld the great white bird soar above the racecourse and pass over and beyond the trees," wrote Peyrey, who was watching from the grandstand. "We were able to follow easily each movement of the pilot, note his extraordinary proficiency in the flying business, perceive the curious warping of the wings in the process of circling and the shifting position of the rudders." After one minute and 45 seconds of flight, Wright returned to the ground, descending "with extraordinary buoyancy and precision," while the crowd in the stand broke into cheers. "I saw the man who is said to be so unemotional turn pale," wrote Peyrey. "He had long suffered in silence; he was conscious that the world no longer doubted his achievements."

Pandemonium ensued. Two small boys, who had climbed a fence to peek, ran to their bicycles and pedaled into Le Mans, squealing at the top of their voices: *"Il vole, il vole!"* — "he flies, he flies!"

The praise for Wilbur's performance and for other demonstrations that he soon gave was unstinting. "I would have waited 10 times as long to see what I have seen today," said Blériot. "Monsieur Wright has us all in his hands." Admitted Léon Delagrange, "Well, we are beaten." It was left to Archdeacon to sound the sour note. Wilbur Wright had done all he claimed, Archdeacon conceded, but the Wright machine appeared difficult to fly and was hampered by its launching system: "I consider our machines superior. In fact, they have wheels and can start wherever they may descend, without the help of rails." But his remarks were drowned out by the cheers for Wilbur Wright.

Next day the hundreds of people who thronged to the race track in hope of seeing a reprise discovered that Wilbur, the son of a Protestant bishop, never flew on Sunday. But the thousands who came on Monday and the following days and weeks to Hunaudières, and subsequently to more spacious grounds at nearby Camp d'Auvours, saw him fly higher and farther until, on September 21, 1908, he set a new world endurance record of 1 hour 31 minutes 25 seconds.

Wilbur's spectacular flights accomplished their basic purpose—to assure the formation of Wright-licensed companies in France and later in Germany and England. But Wilbur's European sojourn was of even greater value to the aviators of the Continent. At last they could see for themselves how the Wrights dealt with the problem of lateral control; the enigma that had retarded European aviation for so long now had

L'AEROPLANE

urnal
ABONNEMENTS
5 CENTIMES
t Journal, 10 cent.
SEINE et SEINE-ET-OISE.. 2 fr. 3 fr. 50
DÉPARTEMENTS.......... 2 fr. 4 fr.
ÉTRANGER.............. 2 50 5 fr.
poste
Numéro 928
908

LBUR WRIGHT EN PLEIN VOL

A Paris magazine cover depicts the sensation caused by Wilbur Wright's first flight in France in August 1908.

been reduced for them to simple mechanics, an elementary arrangement of wires and pulleys. The French lost no time adapting the Wrights' wing-warping system to their airplanes, and for the first time they found themselves truly flying.

Emboldened by this newfound mastery, they began edging warily toward a challenge that had seemed suicidal just a few years before—a flight across the English Channel. Such an adventure was made more attractive in 1909 by Lord Northcliffe's *Daily Mail,* which established a prize of £1,000 ($5,000) for the first crossing of the Channel, between sunrise and sunset, by a heavier-than-air machine.

The inevitable question was asked of Wilbur Wright: Would he be the first man to dare the Channel? Wilbur dismissed the notion curtly. It would be "a useless risk," he said, "nor if effected would it prove anything more than is braved by flying over dry land."

This might well have been true, but Wilbur Wright was almost the only person in aviation who thought so.

Fair weather rarely favors the sullen, gray-green English Channel. One day it is shrouded in fog, the next pelted by rain. And always there is wind, the foe of the early aviator. The wind roars over the Channel, slams into the coastal hills and gusts up in freakish, powerful currents. At its narrowest point, the Channel stretches 21 miles from the cliffs of Dover to bleak headlands on the French coast near Calais.

In July 1909, a few miles southwest of Calais near the village of Sangatte, the popular young aviator Hubert Latham had tarpaulins nailed up as a makeshift hangar for his Antoinette IV—a new monoplane he would pilot in his bid to win the *Daily Mail* prize. Latham had made a private bet of 17,000 francs, about $3,400, that he would not only win the prize but do it by August 1, now just a few weeks away.

On both sides of the Channel, the 26-year-old Latham was everybody's favorite to win. He was French but his forebears were English; he had spent a year at Balliol College, Oxford; his mother's family had ties to German banking interests and he spoke German fluently. He was rich, handsome, a casually elegant man-about-Paris whose personal trademarks, a checked cap and a long ivory cigarette holder, were familiar to every newspaper reader. Women idolized him. Latham had hunted big game in Africa and raced motorboats off Monaco. Early in 1909 he had taken up the new sport of flying and only three months later had established a world's endurance record for monoplanes, flying for 1 hour 7 minutes 37 seconds until a rainstorm forced him down. Once, when asked by the President of France what his career was, apart from flying, Latham replied simply, "I am a man of the world."

With Latham at Sangatte was the designer of both the Antoinette IV and its engine, a huge, red-bearded mountain of a man, Léon Levavasseur. Levavasseur, a onetime artist, had named both aircraft and engine for the teen-age daughter of his business partner, and the plane was as slim and graceful as its namesake.

The Antoinette had a wingspan of 42 feet and a fuselage 38 feet long; its forward half, made of polished wood, tapered back to a spreading, birdlike tail assembly. Its pilot perched half out of the fuselage with a wheel at each side for operating the elevator and the rudimentary ailerons that some designers were now using instead of wing warping to achieve lateral control. The innovative side-wheel arrangement eliminated the steering column and the danger of the pilot being impaled on it in case of a crash. Forward, nestled behind a two-bladed aluminum propeller in the plane's canoe-like prow, was a 50-horsepower water-cooled V-8 engine, very advanced in its conception, with direct fuel injection and a crankcase made of aluminum to reduce weight. (Advertisements in aeronautical journals showed it being lifted by one man.) Although the engine was temperamental, its power-to-weight ratio of 1 to 4 had already made it the workhorse of European aviation.

Through days of rain and overcast skies, Latham and Levavasseur waited at Sangatte. Spectators who flocked from Calais each morning in hopes of watching a takeoff went home unrewarded. Across the Channel in Dover, expectant Londoners arrived by the trainload, while the harbor filled with small boats and a White Star liner delayed sailing for the United States so that its passengers would not miss the great event. When the thick Channel mists unexpectedly cleared on Monday morning, July 19, Latham decided that the time was ripe. Levavasseur boarded a French destroyer waiting offshore and signaled Latham by flag to take off. The destroyer fired a two-gun salvo, indicating it was ready for escort. As his crew restrained the plane's wings and tail, Latham revved the engine and then shot from the bluffs at the water's edge, heading for England. He was seven and a half miles out when the Antoinette engine faltered. Latham watched the propeller slow, then stop. The plane came down from about 1,000 feet, pancaking into the choppy sea. Nonchalantly propping his feet on the floating wooden fuselage, Latham lit a cigarette and waited for rescue.

He arrived back in Calais with a French naval officer's raincoat over his wet clothes, a sailor's hat with a pompon on his head, and his sangfroid undamaged. He kissed a pretty young girl, announced he was going to take a steam bath and then get ready for a second try, with a new plane. "I wasn't lucky this time, but the Channel will be conquered," he insisted. "I'm starting over and I will succeed."

By now, however, Latham had competition. Count Charles de Lambert, an expatriate Russian who had been the first European to take flying lessons from the Wrights, had brought two Wright machines to the Channel coast and crossed to England by boat to scout landing sites. And at Les Baraques, a village between Sangatte and Calais, an unused barn had become a hangar and headquarters for Louis Blériot, who entered the Channel contest within hours of Latham's failed attempt.

Blériot's entry had been made possible only by a last-minute financial windfall. The impulsive aviator had spent both his own fortune and his wife's dowry—altogether some 780,000 francs—on aerial experi-

Portly engineer Léon Levavasseur designed the Antoinette engines that powered many of Europe's first airplanes and fastest speedboats. The engines had a tendency to cut out in mid-flight.

mentation, and by the beginning of 1909 he was bankrupt. His career was salvaged by a fairy-tale stroke of luck. On July 1, his wife had been visiting the relatives of a rich Haitian planter living in Paris when the Haitian's young son climbed onto the apartment-house balcony. Madame Blériot grabbed the child just as he was about to fall off. In gratitude, the Haitian loaned Blériot 25,000 francs for the Channel attempt, but even then, Blériot was nearly broke. "I had to keep going," he wrote later, "because, like a gambler, I had to recoup my losses. I had to fly."

At that point Blériot was barely able to walk, let alone pilot a plane. During a recent endurance competition the asbestos covering his plane's exhaust pipe had torn loose and Blériot's foot was severely burned. At Les Baraques he was hobbling around painfully on crutches; kicking a rudder bar with that foot would be worse. But Latham's crew was working round the clock at Sangatte assembling the new Antoinette VII, and it would soon be ready for another try. Blériot knew he had no choice but to go before the foot healed. "In exploits of this sort, whatever they are worth," he observed, "it's only the first that counts."

His latest plane, the Blériot XI, seemed hardly in a class with the graceful, finely appointed Antoinette. It was small, awkward, underpowered, with only 150 square feet of wing area, a quarter of the Antoinette's, and a 25-horsepower three-cylinder engine that was dwarfed by the Antoinette's 50-horsepower V-8. The Blériot's trellis fuselage was only partially covered and the pilot sat on a wooden seat with a leather strap as a back rest. The airplane had a wing-warping control based on the one Wilbur Wright had demonstrated in France the year before, and no instruments of any sort.

Blériot's chances hung on his tiny power plant; it was the creation of an Italian named Alessandro Anzani, a rough-cut and foulmouthed former bicycle racer who now produced engines for motorcycles. Anzani's power plants were as crude as he was. Their cast-iron cylinder blocks were rough, not even sandblasted. Holes punched in the bottoms of the cylinders let the hot exhaust gases escape and kept the engines cool. The Anzanis rattled incessantly because of "formidable play in their joints," recalled Ferdinand Collin, Blériot's mechanic. "They spit oil out of the holes at the end of every stroke, smearing the pilot with an oily film, so that an aviator had to be heroic as well as long-suffering to keep on flying these miserable mechanisms."

But Anzani engines had one redeeming virtue: They kept running. Blériot had gradually worked up from five-minute flights to a quarter hour and then to half an hour, the point at which he figured he could trust the engine on a Channel crossing.

The July days slipped by and the Channel weather remained blustery. Blériot and Latham waited, each warily eying the other (Count de Lambert, after wrecking one of his planes in a test flight, had dropped out of the race). Latham was particularly edgy; his new Antoinette VII had a wing-warping system instead of ailerons, and he had never flown such a plane before. Nor would the weather allow him a test flight, now that the new plane was ready.

Blériot, on the other hand, knew his plane intimately, but he was less sure of finding a landing place on the unfamiliar English side of the Channel. The beach front at Dover was too narrow, and the famous 300-foot Shakespeare Cliff there was too high—a full 100 feet higher than he could expect to climb in his little plane. A French newsman, Charles Fontaine, assigned by his paper to cover Blériot's arrival, offered to scout the terrain. Beside Dover Castle, in a grassy hollow called Northfall Meadow, Fontaine found a gap in the escarpment less than 100 feet above the water. He bought some picture postcards, marked the spot with an X, and sent them over on the Channel ferry with a note to Blériot saying he would be standing there waving a large French flag.

On Saturday, July 24, the Channel weather was still foul. Wind swept the Calais headlands and roiled the waters offshore. Blériot, who now found that he could sit in the plane and work his injured foot almost normally, gave his engine another trial. He asked Collin: "Well, am I going to make it?"

The mechanic replied: "You shouldn't go, Boss, if you don't feel confident." At this Blériot turned snappish. "I'm not asking about myself. I'm asking your opinion about the machine."

Collin recovered quickly. "There are two things I'm certain of: the excellence and determination of the pilot, and also that the machine is in perfect shape."

That night, both Blériot and Latham went to Calais port to check with their naval escorts. Blériot remained in Calais. Latham returned to Sangatte, but before retiring he left a note for Léon Levavasseur, the Antoinette's designer, who was acting as crew chief: "Midnight. The wind seems to be slacking off. If this continues, wake me at 3:30."

The wind did continue to slacken. At 2 a.m. the sky was clear, the air calm. But it was the Blériot camp that came awake. A car was sent to fetch Blériot from a Calais hotel, while at Les Baraques the engine-maker Anzani contributed to the general excitement by running around in his nightshirt, firing off blanks with a revolver.

Blériot arose grumpily. "I swear I wasn't in any mood to fly," he admitted later. "I would have been happy if they'd told me the wind was blowing so hard there was no point in even trying." He did not feel like breakfast; friends forced him to eat. At dockside, he put his wife on board the French destroyer *Escopette* and by the time he reached Les Baraques he had regained his customary vigor. He roared orders to bring out his plane. "Now I had courage enough for two," he said.

Despite the hour, the darkened farmyard swarmed with curious spectators. The commotion irked Blériot; he would rather have been alone. The plane's engine was warmed up. A dog barked, ran into the whirling propeller and was chopped to a pulp. A bad omen, some villagers felt. It was not yet sunrise, still too early for takeoff, according to the contest rules. Blériot pulled on freshly laundered blue coveralls and a leather

Hubert Latham's Antoinette IV monoplane is fished from the sea by the destroyer escort Harpon after Latham's attempt to fly the English Channel fell short in July of 1909. He survived the ditching, only to die three years later on the horns of a wounded buffalo while hunting in Africa.

helmet. He had his crutches strapped to the side of the plane, tucked a distress flag (to be waved in case he ditched) beside him and took his plane up for a trial spin. The Anzani engine popped noisily but regularly, the plane's new wooden propeller pulled beautifully and Blériot glided back to an easy, perfect landing.

There was a last look with the binoculars, southwest toward Sangatte and the Latham camp. Nothing stirring yet. From the shore at Les Baraques a flag signaled sunrise. Blériot could go. It was 4:41 a.m., Sunday, July 25, 1909.

"Right after I climbed into the plane, I was gripped by an uneasy feeling: What was going to happen? Would I make it to Dover? Just passing thoughts, which did not last long, fortunately," Blériot recalled. "Now I thought only of my machine, the engine, the propeller. Everything was going now, everything vibrating. At the signal, the crew let go. I was up."

Blériot put on full speed to clear the telegraph wires at the end of the field, soared out over the dunes and swung past the *Escopette*. The destroyer's smoke so blackened the sky that Blériot feared for a moment that he had jumped the gun. But the sun had risen, and he settled back to fly the plane. "I went on and on, peacefully, without any feeling, any impression of anything. I felt I was in a balloon," he said later. "As

Louis Blériot, the first aviator to fly the English Channel, occupies a place of honor on a contemporary cigar box, along with a romantic representation of his historic flight.

there wasn't any wind, I didn't have to use any rudder or wing warp. If I could have locked the controls in position, I could have put my hands in my pockets. And the engine, what a marvel! Ah, that fine Anzani of mine, it didn't miss a turn.''

By mid-Channel, Blériot grew almost euphoric: ''The first part had been easy; cake. Not wanting to slow down, I had said so long to the *Escopette* and I no longer had an escort. Too bad. Let come what may. For 10 minutes I kept on, alone, isolated, lost in the middle of that vast sea, seeing nothing on the horizon, unable to make out a ship. This calm, broken only by the roar of the engine, cast a dangerous spell.

''Those 10 minutes were long ones,'' Blériot went on. ''I was happy to see a gray line in the west separating itself from the sea and getting bigger as I looked. No question, it was the English coast. I was almost safe. I headed immediately for that white mountain. But the wind and the mist caught me. I had to fight it with my hands, with my eyes . . . I didn't see Dover. Where the devil was I, then?''

Unaware, Blériot was being swept northward past Dover, toward the North Sea. But again his luck turned; three ships came into view. ''Tugs? Ferries? No matter, they seemed to be heading toward a port: Dover, no doubt, so I calmly followed them. The sailors were cheering me enthusiastically. I almost wanted to ask them the way to Dover. Alas, I didn't speak English."

Blériot flew southward along the forbidding cliff. "The wind I was fighting now caught me worse than ever," he recalled. "Suddenly, at the edge of an opening that appeared in the cliff, I saw a man desperately waving a tricolor flag, out alone in the middle of a field, bawling 'Bravo! Bravo!' I didn't point myself, rather I flung myself toward the ground."

Landing in the violent wind was the pilot's next problem. Each time he neared the ground, a swirling gust would lift him up. "At the risk of smashing everything, I cut the ignition at 20 meters," he said. "Now it was up to chance. The landing gear took it rather badly, the propeller was damaged, but my word, so what? *I had crossed the Channel!*"

On the ground, the newsman Fontaine ran toward Blériot, grabbed him, kissed him soundly on both cheeks and wrapped him in the French flag. It was 5:18 a.m. The 38-kilometer flight had taken just 37 minutes.

"That's it," said Blériot simply. "And Latham?"

"Latham is still at Sangatte," replied Fontaine.

And so he was. For a second time, the favored Latham had failed. Incredibly, he had been left sleeping as Blériot took to the air. Levavasseur had not wakened him; no one had. Only the drone of Blériot's plane heading out to sea had brought the Latham camp alive. Then there was furious activity. Latham struggled into his clothes while his plane was brought out and pushed to high ground at the water's edge; the crowd followed. Latham climbed into the plane—a plane he still had never flown—as the engine was revved up. But an offshore breeze that had risen shortly after Blériot's takeoff had turned into strong, gusting winds, more than designer Levavasseur felt the Antoinette could handle. The plane shook from one sudden gust and Levavasseur stepped up beside the cockpit to forbid the flight absolutely; the risk was too great. The normally composed Latham jumped from the plane and ran to his car in tears. After a few minutes he pulled himself together and, when word came that Blériot had landed safely, sent off a wireless: "Cordial congratulations. Hope to follow you soon."

But a London *Daily Mail* correspondent who saw Latham that morning amid the French crowds celebrating Blériot's victory wrote this description of how crushing Latham's two defeats had been:

"I saw against a background of radiant faces and enthusiastic crowds a tall, slim figure with bent head, quivering lips and hands clenched in unavailing regret for a lost opportunity. His eyes were narrowed to a slit. More than once he brushed away a tear. The extreme tension of the past fortnight had told upon him severely, and this bitter blow coming at the end of it was having its natural, its inevitable effect."

Though he could not be first, two days later Latham gamely took off again for England. This time he was within sight of Dover before the engine failed him once more. He came down hard, gashing his forehead badly, and only a prompt rescue saved him from drowning. ➤➤

First across the Channel

Monsieur Blériot "has impressed me as a personality of immense interest and force," wrote the Calais correspondent for the London *Daily Mail* in July of 1909. "Waiting hour by hour in his windy canvas garage, hoping for a lull in the breeze, his lips tight, his eyes apparently fixed on something far beyond our ken, he seemed the type of man born to succeed."

Blériot did succeed. On the morning of July 25 he took off from France in his 25-horsepower monoplane and headed across the English Channel. Half an hour later a British police constable making his rounds below Northfall Cliffs near Dover heard a whirring noise overhead. "I looked up and saw something like a huge butterfly dart across the sky," he reported. "I telephoned to the police station, and then ran as hard as I could. I came across the flying man in the meadow and he shook my hand in both of his. It was wonderful."

For some it was a cause for concern. The British Baron De Forest warned that Blériot's crossing made it "perfectly reasonable" to expect that England could be invaded from the air. He promptly offered a prize of £4,000 to the first Englishman who could fly the Channel in the other direction, to remind Continental Europe that invasion by air could be a two-edged blade.

But in Dover there was only exhilaration. People clamored for a glimpse of Blériot and his little plane, which soon would be packed for display at Selfridge's famed department store in London. "Everybody was excited to the point of incoherence," wrote one reporter. "The Frenchmen were almost sobbing." And the pilot himself? M. Blériot, described as "the calmest person there," went off to a nearby hotel for a hearty English breakfast.

With his friend Alfred Le Blanc (left) peering over the fuselage, Louis Blériot waits dourly to begin his flight over the Channel. "He just sat there with an expression of tragic intensity on his pale face," wrote a correspondent, "waiting for the chance to do it."

Rising into the dawnlight, Blériot starts the Channel crossing. Before taking off, he pointed a finger toward Britain and said solemnly: "By the way, I suppose that is the direction of Dover?"

Their eyes glued to binoculars, spectators cluster on the dunes near Calais to watch Blériot's progress. He stayed in sight for 15 minutes, then disappeared into the morning haze.

Following on a French Navy vessel, Madame Blériot (right) watches her husband outdistance the ship. She joined him at Dover.

Lounging against his monoplane shortly after his historic flight, Blériot shares the crowd's admiration with his well-bundled wife.

2

The great show at Rheims

Louis Blériot's flight across the English Channel evoked a frenzy of celebration. Normally staid Britain went wild over the new Gallic hero. When Blériot's plane was put on display at Selfridge's department store in London, thousands lined up to get a look at the miraculous machine. From London, Blériot and his Model XI returned to Paris and a reception worthy of Napoleon. The plane was drawn through the city's boulevards like an imperial chariot, with top-hatted dignitaries walking beside it as escorts. Horsemen of the Republican Guard, wearing silver armor, flashed their sabers in salute as Blériot passed. He was honored at banquet after banquet, and the oratorical tributes to him grew ever more grandiloquent.

Editorialists hailed a new world of air travel, one in which, they tirelessly proclaimed, "there are no islands any more." The military implications of Blériot's flight were obvious. He had thrown an aerial bridge over Britain's protective moat, the Channel. In one newspaper cartoon the ghost of Napoleon, who in his time had dreamed of leading an army across the Channel, was shown looking at Blériot's plane in flight and asking: "Why not a hundred years earlier?"

The excitement had scarcely subsided when, just four weeks after the Channel crossing, Blériot flew into the limelight again. This time he was the star attraction in the world's first organized aerial competition, at Rheims, in northeastern France. At Rheims, Blériot had more than Hubert Latham to contend with; his European contemporaries were out in full force. The rich prizes offered by the sponsors of the competition drew 22 participating aviators, most of them French, and many—Blériot, Latham, Henry Farman and others—established heroes on the Continent.

The United States, on the other hand, would be meagerly represented. Only one American laid plans to challenge Blériot and the other Europeans on their home ground. Glenn Hammond Curtiss was unknown on the Continent, but in his own country he carried impressive credentials. Curtiss had first achieved fame as a motorcyclist, winning a number of races and setting speed records. Turning his attention to aviation, he polished his reputation through well-publicized accomplishments as a an engine builder, airplane manufacturer and pilot. By 1909 he had emerged as the leading challenger to the Wright brothers' dominance of aviation in the United States. In time, his name would rank second only to those of the Wrights in the ledger of American air

The Gordon Bennett trophy was the most coveted prize offered at the world's first air meet, held at Rheims, France, in 1909. Its ornate silver representation of a winged figure and a Wright biplane proved ironic when the Wrights' archrival, Glenn Curtiss, won the trophy.

pioneers, but not before a long period of increasingly bitter contention that marked and sometimes marred the early years of flight in the country of its invention.

Glenn Curtiss was just 31 in the summer of 1909, but he seemed older. Lanky and gaunt, with dark, bushy eyebrows and a perpetual frown, Curtiss had nothing of the suave, stylish manner of the gentlemen-sportsmen-aviators of Europe. He spoke little and, on the flying field and off, he was all business. He was considered a mild man by those who were close to him, but in competition he could be ferocious. "I hated to be beaten," he once said.

An obsession with speed had driven him since boyhood. Raised in Hammondsport, a village in the scenic vineyard country of upstate New York, Curtiss dropped out of school at the age of 14 and began racing bicycles at county fairs. Then, like his eventual rivals the Wright brothers, he opened a bicycle repair shop. His urge to go faster led to an attempt, in 1901, to marry a gasoline engine to a bicycle chassis. One of the first engines he used, a crude mail-order behemoth that weighed 180 pounds, was so overpowering, Curtiss said, "it almost tore itself loose from the frame."

Abandoning this unhappy union, Curtiss decided to make his own engines, and from there it was only a short step to motorcycle manufacture. Racing his own machines, Curtiss soon filled a room with trophies;

A carborne Louis Blériot (center) doffs his hat to enthusiastic Londoners the day after his Channel crossing. His aircraft, displayed at Selfridge's department store, attracted 120,000 of the curious.

After a tumultuous parade past 100,000 cheering Parisians, Blériot (standing) accepts the gold medal of the Aero Club of France at a banquet in his honor. A model of his Blériot XI is on the table at left.

in 1907, on the broad, hard strand at Ormond Beach, Florida, he drove an eight-cylinder stretched-out motorcycle to an unofficial world's land speed record of 136.3 miles per hour. Of his vision-blurring dash down the straightaway, Curtiss said only: "It satisfied my craving for speed."

By this time, he had earned a reputation not only as a daredevil racer but also as the builder of one of the finest engines in the country. His motorcycle power plant—small, powerful, yet lightweight—was also ideal for aeronautical use, a fact not lost on a few aerial experimenters in the United States. Among them was Thomas Scott Baldwin, a veteran carnival balloonist and parachute jumper; Baldwin ordered a Curtiss engine in 1903, slung it beneath his dirigible, the *California Arrow,* and in 1904 completed the first flight around a circular course made by any dirigible in the United States.

By 1906 Curtiss was soliciting the Wright brothers for business— writing, telegraphing and finally calling on them in Dayton. The Wrights professed no interest in his engine. They were steadfastly guarding their invention from prying eyes and, though polite, gave Curtiss short shrift.

But other aviation enthusiasts, like Baldwin, sought Curtiss engines. The most significant of these was Alexander Graham Bell, who in 1876 had invented the telephone and had grown rich as a result. Bell brimmed over with scientific curiosity; he was building enormous kites fashioned from hundreds of peculiar tetrahedral, or pyramid-shaped, cells, a construction he thought would solve the problems of heavier-than-air flight by providing inherent stability aloft. The kites led nowhere aeronautically, but Bell was nonetheless impressed with the Curtiss engine that he planned to hitch to them. In July of 1907, Bell invited Curtiss, as a mechanical expert, to join a group of young aerial experimenters who were gathered under his patronage at his summer home in Baddeck, Nova Scotia.

At the urging of Bell's wife, Mabel, the group formally registered itself in September as the Aerial Experiment Association, and Mrs. Bell, who had money of her own, put up $20,000 to finance it. Bell named himself chairman and Curtiss director of experiments. Others in the A.E.A. included two Canadian engineers recently graduated from Toronto University, John A. D. McCurdy and Frederick Walker "Casey" Baldwin (no relation to dirigible enthusiast Thomas Baldwin), and Lieutenant Thomas Selfridge, a United States Army officer intent on making a military career out of aeronautics. Selfridge had been assigned by the War Department, at Bell's request, to follow the experiments.

The A.E.A. started out working with a glider, but its declared aim was "to get into the air" with a practical man-carrying airplane. Its problem was to do this without infringing the Wright patents on wing warping. "Of course we could not use that," Curtiss wrote later, "but we believed there were other ways of controlling the plane." As A.E.A. secretary, Selfridge wrote to the Wrights for information on glider construction. The brothers replied affably enough. But they did not forget Selfridge's approach—later, when a long patent battle unfolded in the courts, they would claim Selfridge had tricked them by saying that the A.E.A. wanted the advice for experimental purposes only.

At the beginning of 1908 the A.E.A. moved its headquarters to Curtiss' home in Hammondsport, on the shores of Keuka Lake. There the pontifical Bell led late-night discussions on everything from aeronautical theory to the sex determination of sheep. Bell's Boys, as they were called, would rise at dawn to catch the early-morning calm they found ideal for flying, while Bell stayed abed until noon, assuring himself of undisturbed sleep by wrapping the telephone in towels.

On March 12, 1908, the A.E.A.'s first airplane, a curve-winged biplane christened *Red Wing,* was tested before a well-bundled audience on frozen Keuka Lake. "It sped over the ice like a scared rabbit for two or three hundred feet," Curtiss wrote, "and then, much to our joy, it jumped into the air." After a 319-foot hop at an altitude of six to eight feet, the plane crash-landed on one wing. "It had taken just seven weeks to build the machine and get it ready for the trial; it had taken just about 20 seconds to smash it," Curtiss recalled. "But a great thing had been accomplished. We had achieved the first public flight of a heavier-than-air machine in America."

Curtiss' claim was outrageous; the Wrights had accomplished much more, much earlier and before reliable witnesses. The A.E.A. had, however, thrust itself into the limelight, and not without some justification,

Glenn H. Curtiss was driven by a self-confessed craving for speed. On a motorcycle in 1907 he set an unofficial world's record of 136.3 mph. Two years later the newspapers hailed him as the "Champion Aviator of the World" for an airborne speed of 46.5 mph.

for its subsequent planes demonstrated the group's steadily improving talent for aircraft design.

The A.E.A.'s next model, called *White Wing,* had wing-tip ailerons to control roll and a new wheeled landing gear instead of skids; it managed five respectable hops. On May 21, at the Stony Brook Farm race track outside Hammondsport, Curtiss flew the *White Wing* 1,017 feet, landing without damage in a plowed field. Immediately a rumor spread—fueled by publication in the prestigious magazine *Scientific American*—that the A.E.A. was going into manufacturing, offering planes for $5,000 each, delivery within 60 days. "They have got good cheek!" Orville Wright observed contemptuously when he read the story.

But for all Orville's pique, the A.E.A. was already threatening the Wrights' position. A new plane, the *June Bug,* the first to be designed by Curtiss, was completed in less than a month, tested and entered in the *Scientific American's* $2,500 silver-trophy competition for the first public flight in the United States over a one-kilometer straightaway course.

The A.E.A.'s unexpected entry put the *Scientific American* in a quandary. The most popular scientific journal in the country, it had been painfully slow in the past to acknowledge the achievements of the Wright brothers. To make amends for this awkward lapse, the magazine's publisher, Charles A. Munn, had established the prize in 1907 as a virtual gift to the Wrights, anticipating that they would step forward and claim it easily. Characteristically, the Wrights showed no interest.

When the A.E.A. put in its bid, Munn wrote to Orville, urging him to enter. Orville turned him down, partly because of Munn's own rule that the takeoff of any contending plane be unassisted. The Wrights were still using a catapult launching system; while they could have adapted a plane for wheeled takeoff, Orville wrote to Munn that they were too busy to make such a modification. The United States Army had expressed interest in buying their invention and Orville was preparing a plane for trials—a venture that had clear precedence over vying for prizes. Wilbur was in France, readying a Wright machine for the demonstrations later that summer that would so impress the Europeans.

So the field was open to Curtiss and the A.E.A.; publisher Munn found himself in the awkward position of accepting their lone entry. Curtiss, with his entrepreneur's eye for publicity, set the Fourth of July holiday of 1908 as the trial date and invited members of the three-year-old Aero Club of America to Hammondsport to watch.

From New York and Washington they came, together with reporters and photographers, to join the crowd of locals who thronged the Stony Brook Farm race track and the surrounding hillsides. The Wrights' flights had been haphazardly witnessed. But these spectators at Stony Brook were the first large gathering of Americans summoned expressly to see a manned airplane fly.

Coatless, with his sleeves rolled up, Curtiss climbed into the *June Bug* and fitted his shoulders into the yoke by which he would control the ailerons. He yelled for the men holding the plane to let go, headed down the track and took off. The flag marking one kilometer "was quickly reached and passed," he wrote later, "and still I kept the aeroplane up, flying as far as the open fields would permit, and finally coming down safely in a meadow, fully a mile from the starting place." Curtiss added that he "might have gone a great deal farther, as the motor was working beautifully and I had the machine under perfect control, but to have prolonged the flight would have meant a turn in the air or passing over a number of large trees."

Like so many of the early European aviators, Curtiss was obviously having problems with anything but straight flight. Yet the *Scientific American* trophy had been won and an ecstatic victory cable went off to Bell at his summer home in Canada. Even though it was a Sunday, Bell wired his attorneys in Washington: Get up to Hammondsport to examine the *June Bug* for patentable features. Pending their arrival, Bell ordered the plane grounded. IMPORTANT TO KEEP MACHINE UNINJURED UNTIL THEN, he cabled.

The *June Bug's* success had an instant effect on the Wrights as well. Within the week, from France, Wilbur instructed Orville to warn Curtiss against patent infringement; on July 20, Orville wrote to Curtiss, reminding him of Selfridge's earlier request for information: "We did not intend, of course, to give permission to use the patented features of our machine for exhibitions or in a commercial way. . . . If it is your desire to enter the exhibition business we would be glad to take up the matter of a license to operate under our patents for that purpose."

Curtiss deflected the Wrights' letter with a qualified assurance that he was not intending to go into the exhibition business. Tension continued between the Wrights and the A.E.A., however, and increased when

Officers of the Aerial Experiment Association join their white-bearded chairman, Alexander Graham Bell, at his Nova Scotia home in 1907. From left are director of experiments Glenn Curtiss, treasurer John A. D. McCurdy, Bell, chief engineer Frederick W. "Casey" Baldwin and secretary Thomas Selfridge.

both Curtiss and Selfridge appeared at Fort Myer, Virginia, where Army acceptance trials were scheduled in September for the Wrights' new passenger-carrying military airplane.

Lieutenant Selfridge, in fact, was to be a member of the aeronautical board appraising the Wright machine. Orville was plainly unhappy at his presence. Though Selfridge was a warm, outgoing man, with the look of a large, friendly puppy, he was still considered one of the enemy. "I will be glad to have Selfridge out of the way. I don't trust him an inch," Orville wrote to his brother in France. "He plans to meet me often at dinners, etc., where he can try to pump me. He has a good education, and a clear mind. I understand that he does a good deal of knocking behind my back."

Nor was Orville pleased to find Curtiss around the test field, even though the New Yorker had been summoned there only to help his old friend Thomas Baldwin solve mechanical problems on a Curtiss-powered military dirigible. It was in this atmosphere of suspicion that tests of the Wright plane commenced on September 3.

All went well at first. Plane and pilot performed superbly in several duration flights, astounding the Army brass with their effortless soaring above the Fort Myer parade ground. Finally, in the late afternoon of September 17, 1908, with 2,000 spectators crowding the field, Orville took Selfridge up as part of a series of tests to demonstrate that the plane was capable of carrying two persons who together weighed at least 350 pounds. For the occasion Orville had mounted two longer, more powerful propellers in an effort to gain additional speed. Eagerly, Selfridge climbed onto the cushioned seat on the wing, at Orville's right. Neither man wore a seat belt—no aviator, anywhere in the world, yet had.

The Aerial Experiment Association's second aircraft, White Wing, takes briefly to the air on May 18, 1908, at a race track near Hammondsport, New York. After the plane's 10-foot-high hop, Alexander Graham Bell announced: "We had the first very promising spring into the air today, showing that the machine will fly."

Glenn Curtiss pilots his June Bug over a measured one-kilometer course on July 4, 1908, to win the Scientific American trophy (inset).

Orville made three laps of the field at about 150 feet. "Selfridge sat, arms folded, as cool as the daring aviator beside him," noted a photographer named W. S. Clime, who was watching from the ground. On the fourth lap, Orville heard a light tapping to his rear and glanced backward toward the sound. Nothing seemed wrong. But within seconds came what Orville later described as "two big thumps, which gave the machine a terrible shaking." Suddenly the plane veered to the right. No question now, they were in serious trouble. Orville cut the power and struggled to control the aircraft.

"The machine would not respond to the steering and lateral balancing levers, which produced a most peculiar feeling of helplessness," Orville would recall. "Yet I continued to push the levers, when the machine suddenly turned to the left. I reversed the levers to stop the turning and to bring the wings on a level. Quick as a flash, the machine turned down in front and started straight for the ground. Our course for 50 feet was within a very few degrees of the perpendicular. Lieutenant Selfridge up to this time had not uttered a word, though he turned once or twice to look into my face, evidently to see what I thought of the situation. But when the machine turned headfirst for the ground he exclaimed 'Oh! Oh!' in an almost inaudible voice."

On the ground almost directly beneath them, the crowd watched in alarm as the crippled plane lurched out of control. One of the new propellers had cracked lengthwise and lost its thrust; the other had run wild and fouled a rear guy wire.

"There was a crack like a pistol shot coming from above," said the photographer Clime. "I saw a piece of a propeller blade twirling off to the southward. I stood riveted to the spot with my eyes on the machine. For a brief period it kept on its course, then swerved to the left and with a swoop backward, but in an almost perpendicular manner, it fell for half the distance to the ground. Then, suddenly righting itself, it regained for an instant its normal position only to pitch forward and strike on the parallel planes in front."

The crash raised an immense cloud of dust that momentarily hid the fallen aircraft from view. Clime sprinted to the wreck, arriving just behind two mounted soldiers. They found Orville dangling from the guy wires. "His feet were barely touching the ground, and his hands were hanging limp; blood was streaming down his face and trickling in a tiny stream from his chin, but he was conscious and feebly said, 'help me.' "

Amid more broken wires, struts and torn canvas lay Selfridge. "He had apparently struck the ground with the back of his head and base of the spine," Clime said. "His knees were slightly drawn up. His face and clothing were covered with blood. He was unconscious and if he spoke at all I did not hear him."

Selfridge died that night, the first person ever to be killed in an airplane. The impact of the American officer's death was felt around the world. In Paris, Gabriel Voisin wrote of "the wings that fly, the wings that kill." Orville Wright came home to Dayton in a wheel chair six weeks

Rescuers try to help Orville Wright and Lieutenant Thomas Selfridge after the crash of Wright's plane during Army acceptance trials at Fort Myer, Virginia, on September 17, 1908. Wright recovered, but Selfridge became the first person to be killed in an airplane crash.

later. He would walk (and fly) again, but his left leg and hip had been badly smashed; they troubled him the rest of his life.

The Selfridge tragedy marred an otherwise golden season for the Wrights. On the verge of complete success, the Army trials had to be recessed until Orville was well enough to resume. But in France, Wilbur's triumph was unqualified. His spectacular flights at Le Mans had made him an instant legend among the French; all Europe, in fact, was captivated by the taciturn Yankee aviator and his no-nonsense ways.

Wilbur's response when invited to make a banquet speech—"I know of only one bird, the parrot, that talks, and it doesn't fly very high"—was quoted endlessly. His hawk-beak profile was caricatured everywhere. Copies of the cap he wore were displayed in store windows, and the frying pan he used to cook his meals in the hangar at Le Mans was reported to have joined the *Mona Lisa,* for a while at least, among the displays at the Louvre.

The French ambassador to the United States declared Wilbur Wright to be the greatest man in France. And when Orville and their sister, Katharine, joined Wilbur after Christmas, the adulation spilled onto them as well. Katharine, earnest and cheerful but rather dowdy, with rimless glasses and schoolmarm clothes, was glamorized into "The American Girl That All Europe Is Watching," as one magazine in the United States put it. In spare moments Katharine learned French and practiced curtsies, the better to greet her brothers' royal admirers.

The rich and the royal flocked to watch the Wrights fly. In the winter of 1909, when they established a flying school at Pau, a sunny resort near the Spanish border, King Edward VII of England came to call. So did Spain's King Alfonso XIII, who climbed on board the plane next to Wilbur but finally acceded to the wishes of the Spanish cabinet, which had beseeched him not to fly. Loaded down with prize money and awards—including gold medals from France's Aero Club and Académie des Sports, Britain's Aero Club and Aeronautical Society, and even from the Society for the Encouragement of Peace—the Wrights sailed home in mid-1909 to receive homage long overdue in their own country. Congress voted them another gold medal, President Taft welcomed them to the White House, and hometown Dayton, which had acknowledged, then nearly forgotten, their pioneering flights a few years earlier, declared a two-day holiday with parades and fireworks in honor of "the world's greatest aviators."

By the time the Wrights returned to America, the rival Aerial Experiment Association had disbanded after the discouraging loss of two key members. Six months after Selfridge's death, Glenn Curtiss began dealing on his own, contracting privately to supply the Aeronautic Society of New York with a training plane. Then, without consulting his A.E.A. partners, he merged his Hammondsport motorcycle and engine plant into a new firm, incorporated in March 1909 as the Herring-Curtiss Company.

Augustus Herring, Curtiss' new business associate, was a braggart

New York inventor who had worked both with Octave Chanute and with Samuel Langley, the prominent Smithsonian Institution scientist who had been the Wrights' foremost competitor until their breakthrough in 1903. Herring came to Curtiss with the promise of investment capital and grand claims of holding important aviation patents, including one for a gyroscopic stabilizer. However, Herring's patent applications had been rejected by the Patent Office and were therefore worthless; when Curtiss discovered this, the Herring-Curtiss association soured and they eventually parted, but not before the firm became the first commercial manufacturer of aircraft in the United States.

The "smallest, fastest and most beautiful airplane in the world"—so the Herring-Curtiss Company touted the biplane that Curtiss delivered in June 1909, for $5,000, to the newly formed Aeronautic Society of New York. For its yellow-doped wings it was christened the *Golden Flyer.* Weighing only 550 pounds, with a wingspan of 28 feet 9 inches and a 30-horsepower four-cylinder engine, it was a dainty little machine indeed. And with its large between-wing ailerons, it could skip around turns as lightly and tightly as any Wright biplane.

For the Wrights, the sale of the *Golden Flyer* was the last straw. Their suspicions about Curtiss were now confirmed; his assurances that he had no commercial aspirations turned out to be false after all. From the Wrights' perspective, Curtiss had begun to make free and profitable use of patents that the brothers had struggled long and hard to obtain. In August 1909, the Wrights filed lawsuits against both Curtiss and his company to stop them from exhibiting or selling airplanes. It was the first shot to be fired in a legal war that would rage for years, embroiling much of the aviation community on one side or the other.

At the moment, however, Glenn Curtiss was undeterred by the Wright suit. He was deep into a project that demanded all his time and energy: building a new plane designed to capture the speed title at the forthcoming air show at Rheims, in France's champagne country.

The Grande Semaine d'Aviation de la Champagne—"the Champagne Region's Great Aviation Week"—was financed by the city of Rheims and by French vintners as a glorious fusion of their sparkling product and the exhilarating new sport of flying. Rheims week—August 22 to 29, 1909—inaugurated an era of ambitiously staged aerial meetings that would flourish until World War I. But none that followed were as grand as the first. Even in an age of social extravagance, Rheims week set a new standard. Warmed to the occasion by Blériot's Channel crossing the previous month, European society in its full finery was drawn to Bétheny Plain outside Rheims to watch the flying men in their first great assemblage.

The premier champagne houses, from Heidsieck to Veuve Clicquot, had put up 200,000 francs ($40,000) in prizes for speed, distance, altitude and passenger carrying. The richest of these events was the Grand Prix, for distance, with a first prize of 50,000 francs. But the most

Yearning to fly, King Alfonso XIII of Spain (left) questions Wilbur Wright at Pau, France, where Wilbur had set up an aviation school in early 1909. Having promised his Queen and Cabinet that he would not go aloft, the King had to be satisfied with a briefing on the ground.

prestigious award was the Coupe Internationale d'Aviation, or International Aviation Cup, a gaudy silver trophy (plus 25,000 francs in cash) for speed, donated by James Gordon Bennett, the freewheeling American expatriate who published *The New York Herald* and its European edition, the Paris *Herald*.

Competing at Rheims were nearly all the leading French aircraft designers and manufacturers. The entries included nine Voisins, four Blériots, four Antoinettes and four Henry Farmans—a panoply that amply demonstrated French leadership in continental aviation. No other European country had yet developed an aircraft industry.

Six French-owned Wright planes were also entered at Rheims, although the Wright brothers themselves had decided to have nothing to do with the show. "I am only interested in building and selling airplanes," Wilbur was quoted as saying. "Let others amuse themselves with races if they want to."

With the Wrights abstaining, Curtiss had become the natural choice of the Aero Club of America to represent the United States in the race for the Coupe Internationale, or Gordon Bennett Cup, as it became universally called. Curtiss' only problem was to produce an engine powerful enough to overcome the edge in speed that monoplanes, particularly Blériot's and the Antoinette flown by Latham, were presumed to have over biplanes. As Rheims week approached, the Curtiss plant in Hammondsport, working night and day under tight security, turned out a 50-horsepower water-cooled V-8 for mounting on a stripped-down version of the *Golden Flyer*. After only a day of bench tests for the engine—there was no time for flight trials—engine and airframe were knocked down and stored in four packing crates for shipment to France. In Paris, still racing the clock, Curtiss hired a fleet of taxis to take the load across town to make the train for Rheims.

"Those few packages?" asked James Gordon Bennett incredulously when he saw what Curtiss had brought with him for the great flying meet. Told that Curtiss was carrying just one spare propeller, Bennett whistled in dismay.

Curtiss arrived in Rheims to find the sleepy old cathedral town bursting with activity. Not since Joan of Arc had arrived there to crown a French king nearly five centuries earlier had Rheims been so excited. On Bétheny Plain, thousands of acres of grainfields had been cleared to build an "aeropolis"—a great complex of hangars, grandstands and public enclosures next to a rectangular 10-kilometer flying course. There were barber, beauty and florist shops, telephone and telegraph offices with direct lines to various European capitals, and a 600-seat terrace buffet where, between events, spectators could slake their thirst with champagne and listen to gypsy fiddlers. They could follow the races by means of a signaling system almost as elaborate as that of a fleet sailing into battle. Colored pennants were hoisted up a tall mast to indicate flying conditions; square, round and diamond-shaped signals hanging from booms showed which prize was at stake; other symbols

were displayed to identify the individual pilots, to mark forfeits or to indicate the seriousness of accidents.

No less elaborate were the trappings of the French gentlemen-aviators. They came to Rheims like knights to a tournament, equipped with spare airplanes, attended by large ground crews and supported by tons of equipment. Gabriel Voisin brought a full field kitchen: stove, crockery, pots, pans, cook and scullery staff.

In contrast, Glenn Curtiss had himself, one plane and two mechanics, yet the shoestring nature of his operation impressed the French. "When Parisians learned that Curtiss had come practically at his own expense, and that he had been doing a lot of hard work in obscurity," an American reporter cabled his paper, "they warmed up to him more than ever, and it is certain that he will be one of the favorites."

For all that, Curtiss was dismayed to learn that his secret weapon was no longer secret. "My own personal hopes lay in my motor," he wrote later. "Judge of my surprise, therefore, upon arriving at Rheims to learn that Blériot, who probably had heard through newspaper reports that I was bringing over an eight-cylinder motor, had himself installed an eight-cylinder motor of 80 horsepower on one of his light monoplanes. When I learned of this, I believed my chances were very slim indeed, if in fact they had not entirely disappeared." Watching his famed French rival out practicing in his new two-seated Blériot XII, with its big British-built E.N.V. engine, discouraged Curtiss even more. One of his mechanics, Tod Shriver, tried to reassure Curtiss by recalling their old motorcycling days. "Glenn," he said, "I've seen you win many a race on the turns." It was sound advice, and Curtiss took it seriously.

Just as the competition at Rheims was about to begin, torrential rain-storms turned the grounds into a morass. Mud squished over gentle-men's boot tops and spattered the ladies' long skirts; automobiles bogged down to their axles. Nevertheless, before the week was over, an estimated half million spectators had turned out; their number included royalty and lesser orders of nobility, visiting statesmen, ambassadors, generals and admirals.

Despite intermittent rain and gusting winds, the air show officially opened on Sunday, August 22. The nasty weather made for an inauspicious beginning. A little R.E.P. monoplane, conspicuous for its bright red paint job and the two balancing wheels at its wing tips, was towed by a horse to the starting line. Engine clattering, it slithered over the field, but its wheels could not escape the sucking mud and finally its pilot retired in despair. A Wright machine made it into the air using a launching rail but soon came down again when its engine quit. Blériot took off in his new plane but flew only two and a half kilometers, not even once around the course, before a clogged carburetor forced him to land. Hubert Latham managed even less.

But by the end of the day, as the sky cleared, the wind died and a rainbow arched over Rheims Cathedral in the distance, seven planes

A cover illustration from Le Petit Journal reflects the enthusiasm of the spectators at the Rheims meet of 1909 but exaggerates the density of the aircraft. Of the 38 planes entered, only 23 got airborne at all during the eight-day meet.

were aloft together. "The air was thick with aeroplanes," the London *Daily Mail* reported in some awe, describing how the machines "wheeled, circled, swooped, vanished and returned with such swiftness and grace" that they offered "a spectacle such as has never before been witnessed in the history of the world."

Spectacle it was, and a dangerous one; it was a wonder that in the week that followed, not a single aviator or spectator was killed. For among the veteran pilots were novices of frightening inexperience.

One youngster, Étienne Bunau-Varilla, had just received his airplane from his wealthy father as a high school graduation present. The pilot of one of the Antoinettes, a man who is remembered only as Monsieur Ruchonnet, did not even know how to drive an automobile and had squeezed his entire flight training into one long weekend preceding the meet. On a Friday, Ruchonnet had sat in an airplane for the first time in his life and had spent 20 minutes taxiing; on Saturday he had made a few brief hops, bending his landing gear in the process; on Sunday, after repairs, he flew again. Two days later, to cap his training, he circled the field on a mile-long flight.

On the first day of competition, Blériot, Latham and a dashing young pilot named Eugène Lefebvre won qualifying rounds for the right to represent France in the Gordon Bennett Cup race. Britain had one entry for that event, Scottish rugby player George Cockburn, flying a Farman. Curtiss, as the sole American entry, held back. "I had just one airplane and one motor," he said. "If I smashed either of these it would be all over with America's chances in the first International Cup Race."

Curtiss had decided not to enter the endurance contests but to concentrate, as he said, "only on such events as were for speed, and of a distance not to exceed 20 kilometers, which was the course for the Gordon Bennett contest." Waiting until late Monday, the second day, to make his appearance, he circled the course in a practice flight at 43 miles per hour—an informal world's record. The next day Blériot wiped it out with a flight of his own at almost 46 miles per hour.

Weather continued to dampen the proceedings, almost ruining the President of France's ceremonial visit on the third day, but during clear periods the crowds got all the excitement they had come for. From Lefebvre there were acrobatic displays as he maneuvered his Wright Model A Flyer over the stands and under other planes in flight, tracing figure 8s, skimming the field and sending photographers sprawling in panic. (Less than two weeks later Lefebvre became the first European to be killed in an air crash; ironically, he was not pushing his plane hard at the time—evidently the controls simply jammed.)

From Latham there were the demonstrations of nonchalant airmanship that everyone had come to expect of him. "On one occasion, when he was overhauling Delagrange on a little Blériot monoplane directly below him," reported the British magazine *Flight,* Latham let go of the controls and raised himself on his hands "so that he was able to lean over and look down on his aerial rival immediately beneath him."

In the grandstand at Rheims an elegant lunch was served daily to the elite of Europe and America. At right, bearded President Armand Fallières of France and his wife brave the mud to congratulate Louis Paulhan (left) on a victory.

On the fifth day, Latham took the lead in the distance trials with a 150-kilometer flight that lasted 2 hours 13 minutes. This performance cemented his status as the ladies' choice among the flying men at Rheims. He landed to a 10-minute ovation from the crowd and was just beginning to describe his flight to reporters when, as the London *Daily Mirror's* correspondent reported, "he was interrupted by two beautifully dressed ladies, who clasped his neck by turns and kissed him frantically." On another occasion, women were seen weeping as Latham's Antoinette was towed back to its hangar with a bent propeller.

Latham's 150-kilometer flight appeared likely to earn him more than mere kisses. He stood to win the 50,000-franc Grand Prix for distance unless the last serious challenger, Henry Farman, could produce a miracle of endurance.

In midafternoon on Friday, the last day allowed for distance flights, Farman trundled out his biplane. In design, it resembled the Voisins from which it derived. Its canvas-covered box-kite tail assembly remind-

Daredevil Eugène Lefebvre, his left wing dipping dangerously close to the ground, races around a pylon at Rheims in his Wright biplane.

ed one observer of a "washerwoman's back garden, with rows of white garments hanging out to dry." But Farman had dispensed with Voisin's stabilizing side curtains between the main wings in favor of ailerons, thus giving the lines of his plane a cleaner, more airworthy look.

Farman's plane crew had been up since dawn installing a new power plant—a 50-horsepower air-cooled Gnôme rotary engine. This French innovation, in which seven cylinders revolved around a fixed crankshaft, was mechanically intricate but weighed less, ran cooler and gave smoother propeller thrust than any fixed-cylinder engine of comparable size yet developed. Its reliability made it ideal for an endurance test.

Never a flashy pilot, Farman took off smoothly and started droning around the course at some 12 feet off the ground, grinding out lap after lap. A stablemate in another Farman kept him company for six laps, then dropped out. Farman flew steadily, methodically and endlessly, until his plane seemed a natural fixture in the aerial landscape. After two hours he passed Wilbur Wright's record of 125 kilometers, set the previous December. After two and a half hours he topped Latham's mark of the day before. The sun set; the evening chill numbed Farman as he sat unprotected on the biplane's lower wing. At 7:30 p.m., official timekeeping stopped but Farman flew on, steering by such landmarks as trees and haystacks and by automobile headlights that were turned on to help him. Finally, he dropped into the searchlight glare in front of the grandstands and landed. The band struck up "God Save the King"; Farman was, after all, British. To the crewmen who sprinted joyfully up to his plane, he uttered one sentence in misery: "I am so cold." Then he was carried on their shoulders to a shed.

The new endurance champion had covered 180 kilometers—more than 100 miles—in 3 hours 4 minutes 56 seconds; he was to be the week's biggest money winner. With the Grand Prix added to a first in the passenger-carrying race and a second in the altitude competition, Farman's earnings totaled 63,000 francs, or more than $12,000.

Glenn Curtiss, in the meantime, remained mostly on the sidelines, saving his machine for one climactic run at the Gordon Bennett Cup. His refusal to compete against the Europeans in the less prestigious contests prompted some rumblings from the large contingent of Americans who were in avid attendance at Rheims, but the single-minded Curtiss paid no attention. Between brief but impressive practice flights he worked intently with his mechanics in a hangar shed draped with the Stars and Stripes. To coax a bit more speed from his plane, Curtiss removed the bulky fuel tank used in earlier trial runs and replaced it with a slimmer, smaller tank; it offered less wind resistance and held just about enough fuel to get him twice around the 10-kilometer course. Curtiss also contemplated a selection of new propellers. Lucien Chauvière, the leading French propeller maker (who not long before had converted his factory from the manufacture of wooden toilet seats) had graciously offered Curtiss a propeller especially crafted for his machine. Curtiss appreciated the gesture but decided to stick with his own.

While the American crew tinkered inside the hangar, smashups multiplied on the field outside. Observing what was happening to his better-equipped rivals only reinforced Curtiss' anxiety over damaging his one irreplaceable airplane. "At one time," he wrote, "I saw as many as 12 machines strewn about the field, some wrecked and some disabled and being hauled slowly back to the hangars, by hand or by horses." Most of the frequent crashes were minor, but a few could have been tragic. One pilot, wobbling to a forced landing, almost clipped a picnicking couple. Blériot, making a trial run with a passenger, smashed into a barrier as the spectators behind it shrieked and scurried to safety. No one was injured, but Blériot's plane was upended and badly damaged.

On the sixth day, the meet almost was marred by a mid-air collision. Louis Paulhan, who had been licensed for a month, took off in a Voisin directly into the path of Léon Delagrange, who was rounding a turn and losing altitude in his Blériot. Delagrange tried desperately to climb but his engine did not have the power. Paulhan went into a sharp dive. He avoided contact but was caught in the Blériot's turbulent prop wash. One of his wing tips caught the ground and the plane crashed. Paulhan was thrown clear; he suffered only a gashed nose and, though badly shaken, was able to walk off the field. But his airplane was a complete wreck, as were his chances of further competition.

The next morning, Saturday, dawned clear and hot, perfect flying weather for the main event of the week, the Gordon Bennett race. Thousands of weekend spectators, anticipating a rousing climax to the Rheims meet, crammed into the cavernous grandstands and overflowed onto restricted areas on the grass, where they argued with gendarmes to keep their places. In the stands, heavy betting commenced. The odds-on favorite was the Frenchman Blériot, but Curtiss, the lone American, was a close second choice.

As usual, Curtiss was out early, hovering over his gold-winged flying machine, tightening nuts, strumming wires, itching to fly before the wind had a chance to rise. As soon as takeoffs were officially permitted, Curtiss, in a leather jacket and visored cap, went up for a trial spin. A weak breeze toyed with the pennants on the signal pole; from the ground, the air looked deceptively calm.

Just around the first turn of the course, Curtiss ran into fierce, invisible turbulence created by thermal updrafts billowing from the hot ground. His plane danced like a leaf in a storm. So violent was the pitching that Curtiss resolved then and there: "If I get out of this alive I will not start again under such conditions for the Coupe or any other event."

Once back on the ground, however, he forgot his resolution the instant he discovered, to his surprise, that his speed for the trial lap had been the fastest yet recorded. "I thought the matter over and came to the conclusion that this disturbed or boiling atmosphere without any wind was conducive to speed," Curtiss recalled. "With the broken air currents the propeller always had a fresh mass of air to work on, consequently obtaining great push."

He decided to gamble on his theory; he would make his bid for the Cup immediately, taking advantage of the turbulence while it lasted. Each contestant was allowed only one try, two laps around the 10-kilometer course. The boiling air—if he survived it—might give him the winning margin of speed.

The judges and timekeepers were notified. The Curtiss crew topped off the plane's new gasoline tank and tested the tension of its guy wires. They spun the propeller, and Curtiss took to the air.

"I climbed as high as I thought I might without protest, before crossing the starting line—probably 500 feet—so that I might take advantage of a gradual descent throughout the race, and thus gain additional speed," he wrote later. Curtiss drove his plane to the limit, as if he were barreling around a motorcycle track. "I cut the corner as close as I dared and banked the machine high on the turn," he said. On the backstretch he smashed into the same turbulence as before. On his previous flight he had eased up on the throttle here; this time he kept it wide open.

"The shocks were so violent indeed that I was lifted completely out of my seat and was only able to maintain my position in the aeroplane by wedging my feet against the frame," he wrote. "When I passed above the 'graveyard,' where so many machines had gone down and were smashed during the previous days of the meet, the air seemed literally to drop from under me."

Riding the elevator hard, Curtiss plunged on through the thermal wall. When he landed after circling the course twice, a mob of cheering Americans rushed over, certain that his time of 15 minutes 50 seconds for the 20 kilometers—46.5 miles per hour—would win. Curtiss was less optimistic. Until his competitors had flown, he would continue to feel, he said, "like a prisoner awaiting the decision of the jury."

Now the wind was beginning to gust. Britain's chance for victory collapsed when Cockburn grazed a haystack during a low turn and crashed. Fighting wind much of the way, Lefebvre's Wright did not even manage 40 miles per hour, and Latham, who followed him, was blown to the wrong side of a pylon and came in nearly two minutes behind Curtiss' time.

All the French hopes now were pinned on Blériot. The conqueror of the Channel spent the entire afternoon tinkering with his engine and trying out propellers; not until 20 minutes before racing ended did he begin his try for the Cup. Blériot had already gambled on one significant change in his airplane: While hastily rebuilding the plane after the crash into the fence two days earlier, he had trimmed several square meters of fabric from the trailing edges of its wings. This surgery would reduce drag and, Blériot figured, would gain him a few extra meters per second. But it would also limit the plane's capacity to lift weight, and he had taken himself out of the 10,000-franc passenger-carrying race being held that same day.

Blériot's sacrifice of lift for speed appeared to be paying off as he blazed alone down the first leg of the course for the Gordon Bennett

A free-spending goad to champions

From his self-imposed exile in Paris, American publisher James Gordon Bennett used his wealth to spur talented men to great endeavors. The donor of the principal prize at Rheims had invested lavishly in such diverse projects as Stanley's search for the lost missionary, Dr. Livingstone; Marconi's development of the wireless; and an attempt to reach the North Pole. Before turning to aviation, he had established prestigious awards for auto, yacht and balloon racing.

"Bennett knew," said one observer, "that it was sport that created the intense energy that in peacetime wins races and in wartime wins battles." Yet he was essentially a man of the 19th Century: Spurning the fast transport his prizes endorsed, he continued to ride about town in an elegant coach-and-four.

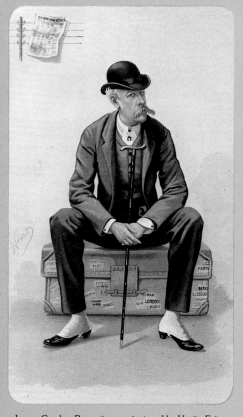

James Gordon Bennett, as caricatured by *Vanity Fair*

A worried Louis Blériot (center, in flying
helmet) watches the competition at Rheims.
Favored to win the Gordon Bennett
trophy with his powerful monoplane, Blériot
ran into rising winds, turbulence and the
inspired airmanship of Glenn Curtiss.

Glenn Curtiss soars past the grandstand
on the day after his hairbreadth victory over
Louis Blériot for the Gordon Bennett
Cup. His Rheims Flyer, the smallest biplane
there, had never flown before the meet.

Cup. Watching from an open touring car with Courtland Bishop, president of the Aero Club of America, Curtiss was stunned as the monoplane flashed overhead. Blériot's first circuit was four seconds faster than Curtiss' time; the Frenchman seemed the sure winner. He sped around again and roared to a landing. Blériot stood up in his plane for a moment, acknowledging a standing ovation from the partisan French crowd. Then he jumped from his cockpit and ran over to the timekeepers' hut. Suddenly the grandstand was silent. Curtiss was puzzled.

"I had expected a scene of wild enthusiasm, but there was nothing of the sort," said Curtiss. "I sat in Mr. Bishop's automobile, wondering why there was no shouting, when I was startled by a shout of joy from my friend, Mr. Bishop, who had gone over to the judges' stand.

" 'You win! You win!' " he cried, all excitement as he ran toward the automobile. 'Blériot is beaten by six seconds!' "

Curtiss, by the narrowest of margins, was indeed the winner. The brass band confirmed it by striking up "The Star-Spangled Banner."

The Stars and Stripes were run up the flagstaff as Curtiss stood by with cap in hand. The French spectators, stunned to silence by the unexpected turn of events, soon overcame their disappointment and joined the American contingent in wild cheering for the Yankee flier, who was soon to be dubbed by the press: ''Champion Aviator of the World,'' a title so recently accorded the absent Wright brothers.

Curtiss' victory was the high point of a pivotal week for aviation, a week in which the world's best airplanes and their pilots for the first time had been tested in competition. If the Wrights had shown men how to fly, the performances at Rheims demonstrated how far man had progressed in mastering this new medium, aviation, in the six years since Kitty Hawk. The competition, moreover, laid to rest any lingering notion that the airplane was only an experimental vehicle of uncertain capability and doubtful future. As one Rheims spectator, David Lloyd George, later Prime Minister of Great Britain, put it: ''Flying machines are no longer toys and dreams; they are an established fact.''

A palatial showcase for the wares of flight

Just one month after the world's first great air meet at Rheims in 1909, an International Exposition of Aerial Locomotion opened in Paris. The number of exhibitors, 333 in 10 categories, testified to the vitality of an industry barely six years old, and the fact that 318 of the exhibitors were from France testified to the dominance of the young industry by that country.

Organized by an industrial association headed by Robert Esnault-Pelterie (whose own aircraft, named for his initials R.E.P., occupied one of the choice positions), the exposition was arranged in the central hall and two great wings of the Grand Palais. The Blériot XI, still oil-stained from its historic Channel crossing in July, faced the main entrance, surrounded by four "stands of honor" displaying other well-known French aircraft. The palace wings

were lined with some 30 more French planes; visitors had to climb a staircase to find a Wright biplane—which itself had been built in France, under license.

Scores of booths displayed examples of the rapid proliferation of products related to aviation: magnetos and carburetors, special clothing and souvenir watches, a lightweight aluminum radiator and even a folding washstand for use in hangars or in the gondolas of sport balloons, which were also on display.

Somewhat nervously, the promoters had flooded Paris with free tickets. But after three days they announced that more than 100,000 people had already attended the exposition, ending any doubt that aviation had excited the imagination of the public as well as that of the businessmen who hoped to be able to profit from it.

French President Fallières (center, with walking stick) opens the Paris exposition near the R.E.P. monoplane designed by the show's organizer.

Balloons loom colorfully overhead in the main hall of the Grand Palais, but visitors appear more fascinated by the powered flying machines below.

Robert Esnault-Pelterie's R.E.P. monoplane, on display in the central hall, boasted internally braced wings and the first fully enclosed fuselage.

The Demoiselle 20, featuring an extremely lightweight bamboo frame, is exhibited above a picture of its creator, Alberto Santos-Dumont.

Henry Farman's pusher biplane was distinguished by its revolutionary ailerons and by its four-wheeled undercarriage of lightweight wood.

Visitors rest for a moment near the star of the Paris show, the Blériot XI that two months earlier had flown the English Channel.

"Already tired of rest, ready to take flight again tomorrow" was one observer's description of the aircraft on display at the Paris exhibition.

A profusion of air spectacles conceived in haste

The success of the Rheims air meet motivated entrepreneurs everywhere to duplicate its spectacle—and if possible its profits. They did not always succeed. One of the first and worst imitations was attempted at Brescia, Italy, in September 1909. When only a few short flights had been made by the third day, troops were required to control the unruly crowd. Two weeks later, at a Berlin meet, disputes between aviators and promoters led to the impounding of three aircraft. It was there that Hubert Latham of France, on striking a lamppost while landing at night, was threatened with arrest for damaging public property.

In October the "municipal sportsmen" of Doncaster, England, as one magazine called them, staged a debacle that the British Aero Club refused to sanction, the weather did not favor and most aviators ignored. The flamboyant Samuel Cody landed in a pothole filled with soft sand and flipped over, Hubert LeBlon just missed crashing into the grandstand and Captain Walter Windham's plane broke apart while being photographed—on the ground.

Despite such misadventures, the aviators remained eager to compete and the public eager to watch. The air show had become an established institution.

An advertised Berlin meeting of "the foremost aviators of the world" was falling flat until Hubert Latham electrified the crowd by flying 6¼ miles across country.

The 100,000 lire in prizes offered in this poster for the air show at Brescia, Italy, could not compensate for the rough ground and poor facilities at the show's site.

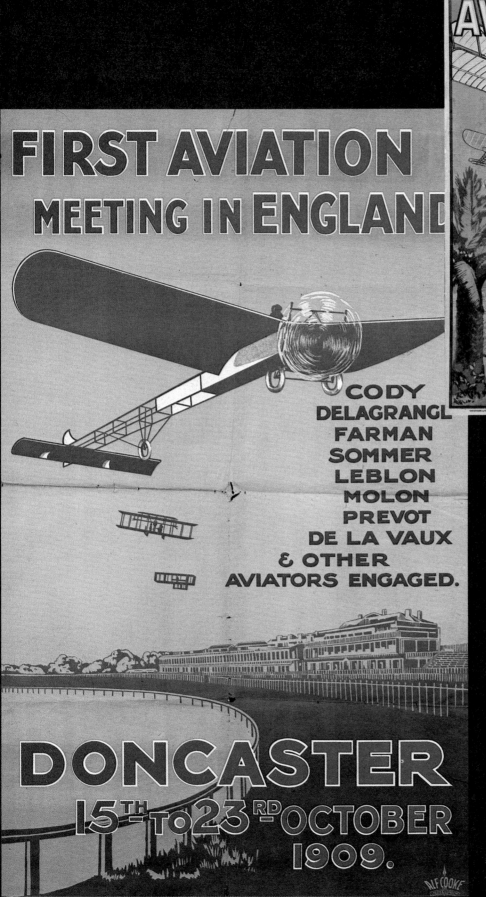

FIRST AVIATION
MEETING IN ENGLAND

CODY
DELAGRANGL
FARMAN
SOMMER
LEBLON
MOLON
PREVOT
DE LA VAUX
& OTHER
AVIATORS ENGAGED.

DONCASTER
15TH TO 23RD OCTOBER
1909.

ALF COOKE

FIRST IN AMERICA
AVIATION MEET

LOS
ANGELES

JANUARY
10-20
1910

American & Foreign
Aviators
DAILY FLIGHTS

The first air meet in the United States, in January 1910, attracted more than 20,000 people each day to the Dominguez ranch in Los Angeles. Dashing Louis Paulhan of France won $19,000 in prizes.

The October 1909 meet in Doncaster, England, conflicted with another held at Blackpool and attracted only five of the eight famous aviators this poster promises.

The Great Aviation Week near Heliopolis, Egypt, in 1910 included the first public flight of the Baroness de Laroche, the first woman to earn a pilot's license.

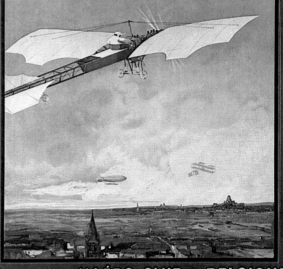

The skies over Brussels look inviting in this poster for the Aero Club of Belgium's royally endorsed air meet in 1910. But a sudden storm caused a fatal crash.

Life imitated poster art at the Rouen meet when Léon Morane, after reaching 951 feet to win the altitude prize, delighted onlookers by flying around the Rouen cathedral.

An advertisement for the aviation festival held at Bar-le-Duc, France, offers dancing, concerts and "various celebrations" in addition to the flying competition.

Organizers of the Milan meet preceded it with the first air race over the Alps. But the death of the victor, Georges Chavez, raised questions about the risks involved.

The first big air show in the Eastern United States offered more than $90,000 in prizes and appearance fees, including $10,000 for a 33-mile race over land and water around the Boston Light.

RAID PARIGI-ROMA-TORINO
28 MAGGIO-15 GIVGNO 1911 - L.400.000 DI PREMI
CROCIERA INTERNAZIONALE TORINO-VENEZIA-ROMA
LVGLIO 1911 - L.150.000 DI PREMI
FESTA NAZIONALE DEI GONFALONI
ROMA·18-19-20 SETTEMBRE 1911
COMITATO FESTE COMMEMORATIVE 1911 ROMA·SOCIETÀ PARIOLI
COMMISSIONE ESECVTIVA DELL'ESPOSIZIONE INTERNAZIONALE DI TORINO
TOVRING CLVB ITALIANO

Airplane and boat races and an automobile caravan are proclaimed in 1911 to celebrate the 50th anniversary of Italy's unification. The second leg of the air race was canceled when none of the Italian entries completed the first leg.

Iᵉʳ GRAND PRIX D'AVIATION
DE
L'AÉRO-CLUB DE FRANCE
CIRCUIT D'ANJOU
ANGERS, CHOLET, SAUMUR, ANGERS

16·17·JUIN 1912
ANGERS

Military observers are shown watching the Circuit of Anjou in 1912. The officers concluded that the fliers' success at carrying heavy loads in foul weather proved "the French Army can count on them."

3
The high-risk pursuit of gold and glory

The successful air show at Rheims set off an aerial gold rush. Promoters on both sides of the Atlantic, sniffing profit in aviation as a spectator sport, hurried to organize aerial tourneys of their own. The shows often were too hastily put together to succeed, but the prize money they offered contestants reflected the phenomenal box-office appeal of the early aviators. By the end of 1909 nearly a half million dollars in purses had been put up. There were rich rewards not only for the winners of speed, altitude, distance and endurance contests but for fliers willing to risk their lives in such crazy—but crowd-pleasing—stunts as landing on a rooftop, flying down a narrow highway flanked by trees or keeping an airplane aloft for at least five minutes with the engine cut.

The lure of flight, or of quick fame and fortune—or all three—was irresistible to scores of adventurous men and women on two continents. Most of them wanted their own airplanes; as a result, the handful of small firms that knew how to build them were deluged with orders.

The Voisin Frères company opened a Paris sales office advertising its biplane as the "most stable of all air machines," adding: "The buyer pays only after taking one flight in the airplane he intends to buy." Stability could not be promised for Santos-Dumont's Demoiselle monoplane, which was advertised as "the fastest, lightest, smallest airplane in the world." The Demoiselle was tricky and dangerous to fly; it landed at almost 40 miles per hour without shock absorbers of any kind (Santos sometimes braked it by grabbing the tires with his gloved hands). Nevertheless, 40 Demoiselles had been sold by the Christmas following Rheims week.

Glenn Curtiss' dramatic victory in the Gordon Bennett Cup race triggered a tremendous demand for his planes and engines. And the economic fortunes of his American rivals, the Wright brothers, were soaring, too. In July of 1909, just before the Rheims meet, Orville Wright completed the United States Army acceptance trials that had been interrupted the year before by the crash that had killed Lieutenant Selfridge. Orville put a new Wright two-seater flawlessly through its paces at Fort Myer, ensuring a $25,000 sale plus a $5,000 bonus for surpassing the government's 40-mile-per-hour speed requirement. In exhibition flying, too, the Wrights were able to command their own price. In October, as part of a fete commemorating the 17th Century voyages of Henry Hudson, Wilbur introduced the airplane to metro-

Claude Grahame-White, glamorously portrayed in Vanity Fair in 1911, blended courageous flying, business acumen and good looks to become Britain's leading aviator and an international favorite.

politan New York. He strapped a canoe between his plane's skids for buoyancy in case of a forced descent on water, then took off from Governor's Island in New York Harbor and flew up the Hudson River as far as Grant's Tomb and back again. For this performance, a New York State commission paid him a whopping $15,000.

Suddenly, the Wrights looked like a very attractive investment proposition on Wall Street. In November 1909, The Wright Company was incorporated with a blue-chip directorate that included August Belmont, Cornelius Vanderbilt, Robert Collier (publisher of *Collier's Weekly* and later donor of the Collier Trophy for aviation achievement) and others of comparable wealth and influence.

The Wrights received $100,000 cash outright, 40 per cent of the stock and a 10 per cent royalty on all planes sold. Wilbur was named president. "A pretty good deal for a 'shy' inventor, reputed to talk so

In the cramped backyard of his Chicago row house, 22-year-old J. E. Mair realizes a dream that was shared by many an aspiring young aviator in 1910.

little," observed an early protégé of the Wrights, Grover Loening.

For a time, the Wrights became the largest airplane manufacturers in the world, with a capacity at their Dayton plant of four planes a month. Meanwhile, Curtiss and a host of lesser American entrepreneurs hastened to capitalize on the popular new phenomenon. The New York *World* reported in August 1910 that the city's business directory, "which two or three years back contained no such word as 'aeroplane,' now has listed more than a dozen firms catering to flying-machine men, and ready to supply anything from an imported Blériot to a home-made pair of ailerons. Aviation competes with the subways, tubes and tunnels as a real estate boomer. Large sections of open acreage on the Long Island and New Jersey flats have been fenced in as 'flying fields' and, as a means for getting land-buyers and home-seekers to look at outlying property, the 'aviation meet' form of advertisement is one of the best that ever happened."

By this time, exhibition teams were being organized to tour the country. During the next few years they would bring the first glimpse of an airplane to thousands of Americans, in cities large and small. The novelty of seeing a flying machine in the sky would not last long, however; the spectators soon were demanding stunts of escalating recklessness for their money. Pilots brave or crazy enough to push their machines to their structural limits to give the crowds what they wanted found that their flight pay escalated accordingly. Some exhibition pilots could earn $1,000 for a day's work—provided, of course, that their planes held together under the strain and they survived to collect. Exhibition flying was a profession that offered young daredeveils adulation and excitement—but an appallingly brief life expectancy.

The business potential of exhibition flying was exploited first by the aircraft builders. The Wright brothers, eager to assure themselves a dominant share of the market, began forming a touring company in March of 1910. To produce the pilots they needed, they opened a flying school. They located it initially in Montgomery, Alabama—to avoid Ohio's winter weather—but their first pupil was a neighbor from Dayton named Walter Brookins.

As a boy, Brookins had hung around the Wrights' bicycle shop watching them build airplanes. He was such a nuisance that the brothers finally promised him flying lessons—someday—if he would leave them alone. In Montgomery the Wrights kept their promise, and Brookins, at 22, proved at once to have such an instinctive talent for flying that the brothers made him their chief instructor.

Glenn Curtiss, too, was teaching pilots who would fly under his banner. His first pupil had been a onetime Harvard student, Charles Willard, to whom he gave lessons just before leaving for Rheims in 1909. His second was a dissolute pixy named Charles Keeney Hamilton, who turned up in Hammondsport later that year.

Hamilton, then 24 years old, was red-haired and jug-eared, with a

Participants in the Wright brothers' first flight school flank Orville Wright in Montgomery, Alabama, in 1910. From the left they are A. L. Welsh, Spencer M. Crane, Wright, Walter Brookins, James Davis and Arch Hoxsey.

deceptive baby face. He weighed 110 pounds—minus the loaded pistol and the roll of bank notes he carried in his hip pockets. He was frequently drunk and often disorderly, he flew with a piece of smoldering punk tied to a strut from which to light his cigarettes, and he hired youngsters to meet him with a drink when he landed.

Hamilton had begun his flying career by jumping out a window in his hometown, New Britain, Connecticut, using an umbrella for a parachute. At 18 he left home to become a carnival balloonist, specializing in heart-stopping leaps out of the basket with five parachutes that he opened and discarded, one after another, until the last chute brought him safely to earth. He graduated to dirigibles and was in Japan, flying an airship across the Bay of Osaka, on the day Blériot flew the English Channel. Hamilton was so impressed by Blériot's feat and the subsequent events at Rheims that he decided to seek out Glenn Curtiss, the American hero of Rheims, and learn from him how to fly.

Curtiss was away when Hamilton arrived in Hammondsport in October 1909. Hamilton appropriated a plane anyway and, without a word of instruction, flew it around the field. Curtiss was not amused at the prank, but he was amazed at Hamilton's natural talent. Curtiss accepted him as a pupil and within a month hired him for his exhibition team.

Hamilton quickly emerged as one of the nerviest—foolhardiest, in fact—of all the early aviators. He would fly anything, anywhere. Once,

Charles "Daredevil" Hamilton, star of the Curtiss exhibition team, displays his flotation gear and ever-present cigarette. Hamilton survived 63 crashes and died, as he always said he would, in bed.

for $10,000, he agreed to fly an airplane up the narrow corridor of Broadway in New York City. The authorities stopped him, but more often than not he flew as he pleased. A series of crashes so smashed him up that, like his planes, he had to be practically rebuilt from spare parts. "There is little left of the original Hamilton," a fellow member of the Curtiss team remarked; Hamilton reportedly had two replacement ribs of silver, a metal plate in his shinbone and another in his skull.

As it turned out, Hamilton was destined to die of tuberculosis, in 1914 at the age of 28. But at that he lasted longer than many other fliers, who died violent and public deaths at nameless flying fields across the American hinterland. So high was the toll that one young pilot, Beckwith Havens, found himself doing double duty soon after joining the Curtiss team in 1910. "We were killing them off so fast that I was beginning to fill everybody else's dates," Havens recalled. "I'd be on a sleeper every night to make the next town, and ended up with three machines and three sets of mechanics. We were so busy that before the season was out I had flown exhibitions all over 13 states and Cuba."

As Havens discovered early in his touring, flying fields were most often chosen by local promoters who, having never seen an airplane, had no conception of the space required to take off or land. "They always seemed to assume that an airplane went up like a balloon," Havens said. "I'd go out to a field with Lou Krantz, my wonderful head mechanic, and Lou would say, 'Can't fly here. Don't you try to fly out of here.' I'd say, 'Let's see. Let's look it over a little bit. Maybe if they took those wires down, maybe if they took a couple of those trees out . . .'

"The people who came to watch thought we were fakes," Havens continued. "There weren't many yet who believed an airplane would really fly. In fact, they'd give odds. But when you flew, oh my, they'd carry you off the field."

Primitive flying fields were hazard enough, but high winds and demanding crowds often proved a lethal combination for the exhibition pilot. Havens narrowly escaped disaster several times while trying to satisfy ill-tempered spectators. Flying in savage winds at Chippewa Falls, Wisconsin, he crashed into power lines; fortunately, the current was off. On another day in Chanute, Kansas, he and his mechanics were slow assembling his plane; they had to fight off a mob that thought Havens was balking. He ended up flying at dusk and landing at last light.

Another brush with surly disbelievers and raging winds came in an exhibition sponsored by the newspaper in Enid, Oklahoma. "The editor met me at the train and took me up to his house for Sunday lunch," Havens remembered. "He told me, 'You know, our people just don't believe it's possible to fly.' With that a gust of wind slammed the front door and blew a picture off the wall. I thought, 'Oh, boy, am I going to have trouble here.'

"They had set up bleachers right out there on the prairie," Havens said. "A big crowd began to gather; as usual, they were skeptical and there was booing. In that kind of a situation we used to try to stall, because usually the wind would go down toward sundown." To kill time and because "all those people hooting at me were making me nervous," Havens started to walk across the prairie looking for gopher holes that might endanger his plane on takeoff.

"I heard a horse galloping after me. It was the sheriff in a buckboard behind a calico pony. He was in a buckboard because he had only one leg—he'd had a leg shot off in a gun fight. He pulled his pony back, looked down at me, and said, 'Son, are you going to fly?'

"I said, 'Yes.'

" 'Git in here!' I got in with him, he pulled the pony around, back we went at a gallop and pulled up to a sliding stop in front of the grandstand. He got up on his one good leg, hitched his gun belt up, held up one arm for quiet and yelled at the top of his lungs, 'Folks, give this boy a chance! This is the last ride he takes before he rides with the undertaker!' With that, everybody laughed. I took off and everything was all right, so I was a big hero—but that's the way it was."

Thousands of skeptical Americans who had never seen a plane fly became believers after attending the first major aerial competition in the United States, near Los Angeles in January 1910. Curtiss pilot Charles Willard had helped to choose the site—the old Dominguez ranch, scene of a Mexican War battle—for its position on a high mesa, where spectators could not see the field without paying an admission fee. Compared with the great champagne aviation week at Rheims, Los Angeles was small beer.

Of a promised contingent of foreign aviators, only Louis Paulhan of France showed up, but he came in force—bringing his wife, two Farman biplanes, two Blériot monoplanes, two student-pilot mechanics and a poodle. Early in his career, Paulhan had worked for Captain Ferber; later he won a Voisin airframe as a prize in a model-airplane-building contest, borrowed the money to buy an engine for it and taught himself to fly. Paulhan had finished fourth among the prizewinners at Rheims. That and his cheerful manner (plus an attractive wife) made him the drawing card the show's promoters were counting on.

The Wright brothers, who had chosen not to compete at Los Angeles, nevertheless cast a long shadow on the proceedings. The moment Paulhan stepped off the liner from France, lawyers in New York served papers informing him that the Wrights had filed for an injunction to keep him from flying in the United States. The control systems of his airplanes, the Wrights contended, infringed their wing-warping patents.

Moreover, a week before the Los Angeles meet began, a federal judge granted the Wrights' request for an injunction against Glenn Curtiss for similar patent violations. Curtiss posted a bond, appealed the ruling and, in the face of possible legal repercussions, decided to ship his planes to Los Angeles.

The Curtiss team collected its share of prizes, $10,250 worth, in the days that followed, but it was "the wonderful little Frenchman," as the

Taking the knock out of hard knocks

The death of Thomas Selfridge in 1908 was followed by three more aviation fatalities in 1909, and by 1910, when 31 deaths occurred, safety had become a crucial issue. Louis Blériot's technique of rolling onto a wing to cushion a crash did not work in heavier, faster planes.

Seat belts, installed in few early aircraft, became more widely used after

British inventor W. T. Warren in 1912 demonstrates the

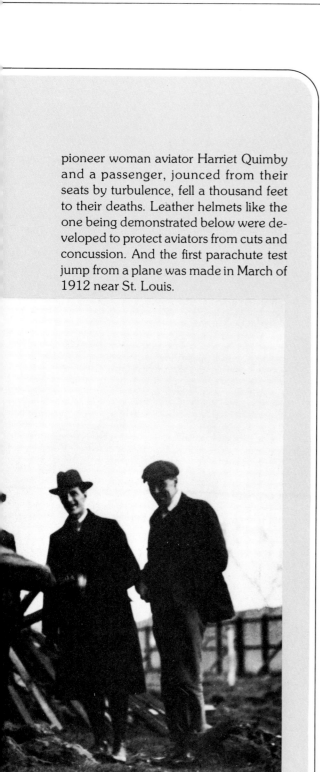

pioneer woman aviator Harriet Quimby and a passenger, jounced from their seats by turbulence, fell a thousand feet to their deaths. Leather helmets like the one being demonstrated below were developed to protect aviators from cuts and concussion. And the first parachute test jump from a plane was made in March of 1912 near St. Louis.

shock resistance of a helmet equipped with springs.

press tagged Louis Paulhan, who outshone the field at the Dominguez ranch. In a sturdy and reliable Farman, Paulhan climbed to a new world's altitude record of 4,165 feet; later he made a sensational 45-mile flight to the Santa Anita race track and back. His $19,000 winnings for the week topped those of everyone else.

Paulhan and his entourage then embarked on an exhibition tour of Western cities. But on February 17 a federal judge granted the Wrights' injunction; a United States marshal who had been shadowing Paulhan served papers demanding that he post a $25,000 cash bond for any flying for profit he did during the next month.

Furious, Paulhan canceled his exhibition dates and stormed back to New York, where he thumbed his nose at the Wrights by flying a few times free to the public. Then he sailed for Europe. Soon he was making headlines again, in pursuit of the richest aviation prize yet offered.

When, in 1906, the London *Daily Mail* had put up £10,000 for the first flight between London and the industrial city of Manchester, 185 miles away, the newspaper might as well have proposed a race to the moon. At that time only one aviator in Europe, Santos-Dumont, had coaxed a flying machine into the air, and his flight had covered barely 700 feet.

By early 1910, however, the stunning progress in aviation had put the *Daily Mail's* prize within reach. The first to bid for it was a dashing young Englishman, a newcomer to aviation named Claude Grahame-White.

Grahame-White might be called the ultimate sportsman. Tall and handsome, well turned-out and a master of society's graces, he was as skillful behind the wheel of a racing car as he was at ease at the gaming tables of Monte Carlo. But he was also a hard-driving businessman who had started his own automobile agency in London's fashionable Mayfair district and had prospered apace. ("Hustle like hell" and "Do it now" read signs in his office.)

Grahame-White's interest in aviation was aroused in the summer of 1909 by Blériot's Channel crossing. The young automobile dealer devoured press accounts of the flight and went to see Blériot's machine at Selfridge's department store. A few weeks later he packed his bag and headed for the aviation meet at Rheims as a spectator, warning his employees as he departed, "Don't be surprised if I come back flying."

As good as his word, Grahame-White talked his way into the forbidden pilots' enclosure and hangar area at Rheims, introduced himself to the aviators, examined their planes and finally ordered one from Blériot. After the meet ended he spent the next eight weeks at the Blériot factory in Paris, helping to build his plane. When it was ready he made a few ground runs, then soloed without taking a lesson.

By February 1910, Grahame-White had opened a flying school at Pau, the fashionable resort town in southern France, with six Blériot XI training planes and eight pupils. He planned to transfer the operation to England in the spring, and to provide the publicity he needed to launch the school there, he entered the London-Manchester race.

According to the rules laid down by the *Daily Mail*, the 185 miles to Manchester had to be covered in 24 hours or less, with no more than two stops en route. That seemed too difficult a task for the little Blériot and its Anzani engine. So after shopping around, Grahame-White purchased another French plane, a Farman with a Gnôme rotary engine. He took a half hour of ground instruction at the Farman factory, flew the new biplane for 80 minutes and pronounced himself ready.

Early on April 23, 1910, Grahame-White took off from an abandoned agricultural showground west of London in pursuit of the prize. After two hours he made his first stop at Rugby, having covered 83 miles. But on the next leg he was confronted by icy head winds that rocked his craft and at times reduced his ground speed to 10 miles per hour; Grahame-White struggled to stay in the air and slowly ticked off the miles. After another hour the plane's engine developed valve trouble and he was forced to come down near Lichfield. But the problem was soon fixed and he was only 68 miles short of his goal. He now seemed certain to go the distance. While waiting for the winds to die down a bit, Grahame-White had lunch in a hotel and took a nap, counting on a relatively easy final leg to Manchester before sundown.

As he slept the weather deteriorated; he woke at 4 p.m. to find the skies black and the wind at gale force. That evening and through the night Grahame-White waited in vain for a break in the storm. Finally he had to accept the fact that the weather had beaten him. There was no chance of his finishing the race within the prescribed 24 hours. The next day, the wind got in a final stroke, overturning his loosely tethered plane, shredding the wing fabric and splintering spars and struts. By the time he got it back to London and repaired, to begin again, Louis Paulhan had arrived to challenge him for the *Daily Mail* prize.

Paulhan's Farman had a slightly different wing and tail configuration from Grahame-White's, but otherwise the airplanes were alike. The imminent confrontation of the two men—one British, the other French, flying evenly matched machines in the world's first cross-country air race—stirred the patriotic blood of two nations. The pressure on Grahame-White, representing the home country, was more immediate. One Briton telegraphed him: "Every Englishman is watching you. Win the race for the honour of Old England."

Grahame-White's luck, however, continued to run thin. Late on the afternoon of April 27 he was napping, exhausted from two nights and days of steady work to complete the repairs on his damaged airplane, when a mechanic burst into his hotel room on the outskirts of London with galvanizing news: At an airfield north of the city, Paulhan had taken advantage of a sudden calm in the blustery weather and taken off. Grahame-White was on the move at once, but more than an hour passed before he was able to follow Paulhan into the air.

A special train, with a white signal cloth flapping from the rear car, was guiding Paulhan over the unfamiliar route to Manchester. Madame Paulhan, leaning from a train window, tried to help by waving a handkerchief. Inside, Henry Farman, who had come over for the event, sat with map and chronometer, while reporters scribbled telegrams to their newspapers and pitched them onto station platforms as the train sped through. Paris, London and other world capitals hung breathlessly on these bulletins of the aviators' progress; in Russia, even the Czar was kept informed. In New York, the *Evening Post* came onto the streets hailing the race as being "not of the century, but the centuries."

Paulhan's lead of 71 minutes was cut to 65 as Grahame-White pushed his Farman to speeds of 35 to 40 miles per hour. But it was not enough. As night fell, Grahame-White landed in a field outside the village of Roade and went to a home nearby for bacon and eggs. Some 57 miles ahead, at Lichfield (where Grahame-White had been stopped on his first try), Paulhan too came down for the night. After a late-evening council of war with friends and reporters, Grahame-White made a bold decision: He would fly by night to overtake Paulhan.

It was a chancy move. Henry Farman had flown into the dusk at Rheims (and in California Charlie Hamilton, for a lark, had once buzzed Madam Tingley's Theosophical Temple at midnight), but no flight over miles of darkened, unmarked countryside had ever been attempted before. Grahame-White had no altimeter; no horizon would be visible, and if his engine should quit, he would be helpless in the black sky.

At 2:54 a.m., with automobile head lamps and bicycle lanterns shining on a hedgerow that he had to clear on takeoff, Grahame-White revved up the Gnôme rotary. At a crossroads ahead, two friends waited to guide him in a steam-powered White touring car. "Presently we heard a far-off drone," one of them recalled. "It grew louder. Then, just away across the fields, low down, we saw a ring of fire moving through the darkness. For an instant I did not understand it. Then I realized it was the exhaust of the revolving Gnôme, flame red against the night, that was causing that eerily moving ring of light. There was the aeroplane, like some big night bird. On it came. I could see the pilot's figure silhouetted between the wings. He waved an arm in greeting and, still continuing to overtake us, was for a spell almost immediately above our heads as we rushed down the road."

Now it was Paulhan's turn, in his hotel in Lichfield, to be aroused from sleep with the word that his rival had stolen a march on him. It was after 4 a.m. when the Frenchman got airborne, again guided by his special train. Grahame-White, meanwhile, was battling winds that rose with the approach of dawn and grew stronger as the darkness changed to daylight. His machine "jumped and danced" violently, he reported later, repeatedly spinning him around so that once he was heading back for London. Finally there was no longer any point in continuing; exhausted from wrestling the controls, Grahame-White called it quits. He put the plane down in a field near a railway line, jumping out to hold it against the wind until his friends arrived to help.

Some 40 miles ahead, Paulhan, the more experienced pilot, was trying to climb above the dangerous gusts. "My machine rose abruptly, then dropped again so rapidly that I was almost jerked out of the driving seat," he recalled. "My arm ached from operating the control lever. I soared up to more than a thousand feet in the hope of finding quieter air, but still the wind pursued me." Paulhan hung on, and at 5:25 a.m. spectators who had been waiting outside Manchester all night saw him in the sky as he began to circle for a landing. Numb with cold, he climbed from the cockpit swearing never to try anything like it again, "not for ten times £10,000."

The London-Manchester flight impressed even Wilbur Wright. Normally a careful man with his words, Wilbur declared his belief "that an aeroplane with sufficient gasoline capacity to attempt a transatlantic flight can now be built."

Wilbur's prophecy of ocean flight was several years premature, but the challenge of long-distance flying had caught the fancy of public and aviators alike. A month after Paulhan landed at Manchester, Glenn Curtiss won a $10,000 prize offered by the New York *World* by flying 152 miles down the Hudson River from Albany to New York City with two stops en route—the longest flight yet made in America.

In June 1910, Charlie Hamilton topped this, flying Curtiss' old Rheims racer from New York to Philadelphia and back in a single day, with a stopover for lunch. The only mishap during Hamilton's 172-mile round trip occurred on the return leg, when he landed with spark-plug trouble in South Amboy, New Jersey, and broke his propeller. Curtiss came down from New York by automobile with a new blade and Hamilton finished the course, winning another $10,000 for the Curtiss team.

That same month Charles Rolls, a wealthy young English automobile manufacturer who had first sampled flight as a balloonist, flew a British-built Wright plane across the Channel from Britain to France and back nonstop. (A month later, while practicing for a spot-landing contest at an air meet in Bournemouth, Rolls was killed, becoming England's first aviation fatality.)

The next big challenge was a mountain chain, the Alps, and in the summer of 1910, as prelude to an air meet to be held in Milan, Italian promoters posted a prize of 70,000 lire ($14,000) for the first flier to negotiate the Simplon Pass, 6,600 feet high, between Brig, Switzerland, and Domodossola, Italy.

Thirteen aviators declared for the contest. The race committee, after looking at their flying credentials, trimmed the list to five—and three of those dropped out. That left only a Haitian-born American, Charles Weymann, and a Peruvian, Jorge Chavez Dartnell, who had been born in Paris and was known in France as Georges Chavez.

Chavez at 23 was athletic and apparently without fear. Two weeks before the Alpine race he had taken his Blériot XI up to 8,487 feet, the highest anyone had yet flown. At that altitude he could clear the Simplon Pass, but threading his way in high winds between the jagged peaks that towered on both sides was another matter.

Aloft before dawn, Louis Paulhan (inset) departs Lichfield on April 28, 1910, on the second leg of the London-to-Manchester race.

The first day of the week designated for the race, Sunday, September 18, 1910, was wasted—it was a Swiss holiday and the authorities at Brig forbade all flying. That day unfortunately ended a long spell of clear weather. For the next four days, one end of the pass or the other was socked in. Chavez went up once in the Blériot for a look and came down shaken: "The machine, it was like a toy in that wind," he said.

Weymann made three tries in his Farman, but each time the carburetor iced within minutes, the engine lost power and he could not climb high enough. Meanwhile, Chavez, scouting the route over the pass by car, was growing visibly more jittery. "Is our equipment really ready for stunts like this?" he asked a friend.

The answer came during Chavez' final flight, on September 23. Taking off in early afternoon from a hillside at Brig and climbing through the gorges to the top of the pass, Chavez sailed over the heads of officials and tourists watching from the summit. He headed southeast, past Monte Leone (11,600 feet) and Hübschhorn (10,400 feet) through the narrow, winding Gondo Ravine toward Italy. From the ground, Chavez was seen hanging onto the controls as his plane tossed violently.

Some 40 minutes after takeoff the Swiss police telephone in Brig began to ring with ecstatic messages from the Italian side: Chavez was over Domodossola, he was heading for a field just outside town, he was landing. Then, as a friend who was watching Chavez' approach recounted later, his plane simply folded under the strain: "He was going to land when he saw a little road blocking the route. He gave it gas again to get past this little obstacle. Then something happened that froze me in horror. I saw the two wings of the monoplane suddenly flatten out and paste themselves against the fuselage. Chavez was about a dozen meters up; he fell like a stone."

With both legs broken and with massive internal injuries, Chavez clung to life for four days; during his conscious moments he was heard to mutter the Spanish phrase that became his memorial: *"Arriba, siempre arriba"* ("Higher, always higher").

In the months following the London-Manchester race, Grahame-White, the gallant loser, basked in his newfound fame as Britain's most admired aviator. He was in constant demand as an exhibition pilot; his good looks and charm were magnetic, his enthusiasm captivating. Grahame-White always seemed to be the first to take off and the last to land. Undaunted by wind, rain or fog, he flew eagerly on days when his fellow aviators were reluctant to leave the ground.

Word of the Englishman's prowess spread across the Atlantic, and a group of Bostonians decided to offer him $50,000 plus expenses to appear in September of 1910 at an air meet, organized by the newly formed Harvard Aeronautical Society, to be held at Squantum, a village south of Boston on Quincy Bay. Grahame-White eagerly accepted.

The Harvard-Boston meet, coming at the end of the summer season at the fashionable seashore resorts nearby, attracted a number of celeb-

In this 1910 illustration for a Milan newspaper, hikers cheer Georges Chavez in his Blériot monoplane as he becomes the first aviator to fly over the Alps. As Chavez prepared to land in Italy, the wings of his plane collapsed and he was killed.

The world's first mid-air collision mars the Milan air meet of 1910 as an Antoinette monoplane (top) flown by René Thomas of France rams England's Bertram Dickson in a Farman biplane. Although they were seriously injured, both pilots survived.

rities. President William Howard Taft came to look, but prudently—as he weighed 300 pounds—declined Grahame-White's invitation to fly. Instead, Grahame-White took up the Mayor of Boston, John "Honey Fitz" Fitzgerald. Also in the crowd, craning to see the aviators perform in the first major air show on the American East Coast, was a rising young New York politician, Franklin Delano Roosevelt.

But the main attraction was Grahame-White. Society beauties vied for rides with him, paying $500 for two or three turns around the field. A woman reporter warned her male readers: "If you want your lady-loves' hearts true to you, it's hardly safe to amuse them by taking them out to the aviation meet. Before you know it these hearts may be fluttering along at the tail of an aeroplane, wherein sits a daring and spectacular young man who has won the title of matinee idol of the aviation field, Grahame-White."

In the air, Grahame-White lived up to his billing. Wilbur Wright, belatedly overcoming his distaste for these well-paid aerial circuses, had come to Boston with an exhibition team; so had Glenn Curtiss. But Grahame-White, flying a 50-horsepower Blériot in the speed races and a Farman in other contests, thoroughly outclassed the Americans. He won first prizes for speed, landing accuracy on wheels and shortest takeoff (26 feet 11 inches), and he picked up $10,000 for making two round trips from the field at Squantum to the Boston Light and back—a 33-mile course over land and water that both Wright and Curtiss deemed too dangerous to try. Grahame-White also won the "bombing" contest, scoring the most hits with plaster-of-Paris bombs on a mock warship. After the meet was over, he raced Glenn Curtiss three laps around the field and won again, adding a challenge trophy to the sponsor's $50,000 guarantee and his total prize money of $22,100.

From Boston, Grahame-White launched a brief but triumphal tour. He went first to nearby Brockton, where the city fathers paid him another $50,000—even though bad weather cut the full week of flying he had contracted for to a single flight. On an October morning in Washington, D.C., he circled the Washington Monument and the Capitol dome and put his Farman down to a perfect slow landing between cast-iron lampposts on the street beside the White House. President Taft was away, but Admiral George Dewey, the hero of Manila Bay, turned out with other distinguished personages to pump the English aviator's hand and watch him rattle down the same street for a successful takeoff.

The dazzling Englishman then made his way to New York City to take part in the biggest air meet to be held in the United States thus far, at Belmont Park race track on nearby Long Island. He took New York by storm. Broadway shows stopped when he entered a theater, and he was led onstage to be introduced to the audience. His romance with actress Pauline Chase, the "Pink Pajama Girl" of the hit production *Liberty Belles*, was front-page news.

Grahame-White continued to make headlines during his New York stay, although not all of them were friendly. He soon found himself

Building a show from the ground up

One reason many early air shows were financial disasters—losses at English meets alone in 1910 were estimated at half a million dollars—was that the organizers seldom anticipated the enormous effort required to prepare the sites. Grading access roads, building hangars and grandstands, removing obstacles and leveling several square miles of ground could cost as much as $100,000.

When the Harvard Aeronautical Society realized that the university's athletic fields were inadequate for its meet in September 1910, it had just three weeks to prepare an alternate site: a marshy field southeast of Boston, near the village of Squantum. These photographs show how it was done. The field later became a naval air station.

An ax-wielding workman clears a tree from the airfield-to-be.

A wooden grandstand takes shape at the field's edge.

A Burgess-Curtiss biplane is assembled (left) on the grass floor of one of the two 50-by-500-foot hangar tents provided by the organizers of the show.

Painters prepare signs to identify aviators and events.

Mechanics sleep in one of the hangar tents, near their work.

embroiled in a bitter international row over the outcome of one of the premier events of the Belmont Park meet.

The entire meet, in fact, was marked from the outset by controversy. The Wright brothers had patent-infringement suits pending in both France and Germany, as well as in the United States, and were making such stiff demands for royalties on all exhibition flights in America that for a time European aviators threatened to boycott the meet. The promoters finally satisfied the Wrights with a payment of $20,000, and the show went on. Later, the Wrights claimed they had been verbally promised an additional $15,000 and tried to impound $198,000 in gate receipts pending payment. (The courts dismissed that suit.)

Further controversy erupted over the route planned for the renewal of the Gordon Bennett Cup race, 20 laps around a tight five-kilometer course (five times as long as the original race at Rheims the year before) studded with trees, telegraph poles, buildings and similar hazards. One corner, immediately dubbed "Dead Man's Turn," offered only 100 feet of flying room between pylon and grandstand. Surveying this gantlet, the Europeans present were aghast. Hubert Latham called the course "suicide." Alfred Leblanc and three other Frenchmen flying Blériots stayed out of the early events in protest.

For his bid to win the Gordon Bennett Cup, Grahame-White had ordered the fastest Blériot yet built, with a 14-cylinder Gnôme rotary

Ralph Johnstone in a Wright biplane completes a "bombing" run over a mock battleship at the Boston air meet of 1910. Military observers were intrigued when Claude Grahame-White, on the first day, scored nine straight hits on the model ship with bombs made of plaster.

engine capable of 100 horsepower. His American rivals, aching to make up for being outshone at Boston, also came well prepared.

The Wrights brought several planes, including a model with the elevator in the tail and with wheels rather than skids. The Baby Grand, as it was called, boasted a 60-horsepower V-8 engine, twice as powerful as any previous Wright machine. On a trial run, Orville Wright flew around the course at an estimated 70 miles per hour; immediately the Baby Grand became odds-on favorite in the speed contests.

Curtiss uncrated a surprise: his first machine "of the monoplane type," as he described it. Actually, it was an untested hybrid of biplane and monoplane, with a 30-foot lower wing and a stubby upper wing that was hardly more than a canopy over the pilot's head. After surveying the competition, however, Curtiss decided not to defend his title in the Gordon Bennett race. "I don't call it sport to send a man up to make a monkey of himself," Curtiss declared. His new plane never flew at Belmont Park.

But there were more than enough aviators—27 in all—to fill the gap left by Curtiss. Among them were the young American millionaire Clifford Harmon and an expatriate American from Philadelphia's Main Line, J. Armstrong "Chips" Drexel, whom Grahame-White had taught to fly earlier in the year at Pau. Also on hand was Charlie Hamilton—described by one newspaper as "limping, scarred and speaking with an impediment on account of an injury to his jaw." The injury was the result of a smash the preceding month at the California state fair, when a burst radiator had nearly scalded him to death. After a spat with Curtiss over money, Charlie was now flying his own biplane, a machine copied liberally from Curtiss' designs.

Freelancing with his own Blériot was another expatriate American, John Moisant, who had recently made headlines by completing the first Paris-to-London flight with a passenger.

Aviation was attracting its full share of eccentrics, and John Moisant was one of them. Still a bachelor at the age of 37, he was rugged, tanned and nearly bald, and his looks fitted his reputation as a Central American adventurer with a taste for revolutionary intrigue. John was one of three Moisant brothers, United States citizens of French-Canadian origin; they had been bankers and sugar planters in El Salvador, where their fortunes tended to rise and fall according to their relations with the current dictator. The other two brothers, George and Alfred, had been jailed for a time for plotting against one Salvadoran despot. Hoping to overthrow the regime and free his brothers, John on two occasions led waterborne raiding parties from neighboring Nicaragua. One attempt failed when his motley band panicked under fire after making a landing; the other effort expired at sea when a patrolling United States Navy cruiser threatened to blow Moisant's flotilla out of the water if it did not come about.

The brothers eventually were released, but with the Central American political climate growing too hot for comfort, John Moisant retreat-

Aviation takes to the footlights

Two days after the Harvard-Boston air meet opened in September of 1910, the first stage play about aviation, a dramatic comedy coproduced by George M. Cohan, made its debut at the Tremont Theatre in Boston.

The hero of *The Aviator,* drawn into claiming that he is a qualified pilot, finds he must either prove it by flying a race or else lose his girl. His triumph over trepidation provided the laughs, while the simulation of flight on stage—using a real Blériot monoplane—provided the spectacle that made the play a popular success in Boston, and later in New York, Philadelphia and Chicago.

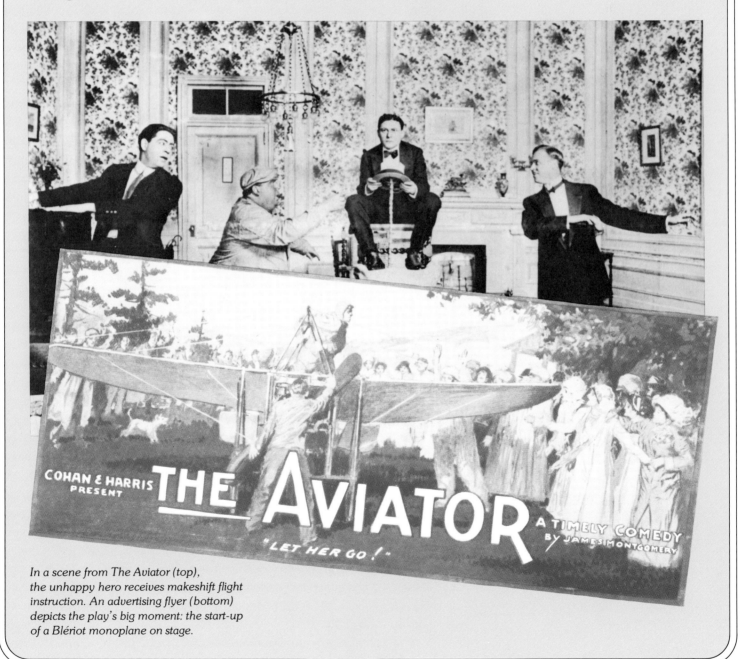

In a scene from The Aviator (top), the unhappy hero receives makeshift flight instruction. An advertising flyer (bottom) depicts the play's big moment: the start-up of a Blériot monoplane on stage.

ed to Paris. With money to burn and time on his hands, he turned to building airplanes. His first, a curved-winged monoplane that he called the Crow, was barely flyable. The second was a biplane with an upper wing made of corrugated metal "like that used in covering certain roofs," as one Frenchman recalled. It roared down the runway "with the noise of a steamroller"—and with about as much lift.

Wisely, Moisant decided to buy a two-place Blériot. The second day he had it, he qualified for his license. Three days later, he flew over Paris. Then he made the flight from Paris to London, with his mechanic as passenger. It took them three weeks—two days to reach the English coast and 19 days, with delays for repairs, to cover the remaining 30 miles to London. It was a slow trip, but it won Moisant a place as alternate on the United States team for the 1910 Gordon Bennett race.

The Belmont Park meet began in a downpour. The handful of hardy aviators who braved the weather on the first day listened helplessly as their engines coughed, sputtered and died with drowned ignitions. Grahame-White draped a blanket over his engine and put a heater under it; thus pampered, it finally came to life and, characteristically, he was the first into the air. On subsequent days, as the weather improved, there often were as many as three or four airplanes aloft at the same time—once a full dozen—and enough aerobatics to keep the crowds morbidly on edge.

Charlie Hamilton's trick landings wrenched screams from the audiences. One fellow pilot recalled: "He would be up about 200 feet and point his nose straight down, just like a power dive; at about five feet from the ground he would straighten up, and stop right on the line in front of the grandstand. People used to think it was wonderful."

The standouts on the Wright team—the "Heavenly Twins," or "Stardust Twins," as the newspapers came to call them—were Arch Hoxsey, aged 26, and Ralph Johnstone, 24. Hoxsey, slim and dapper, a talented automobile mechanic and professional driver, had seen the Los Angeles air meet in January and immediately headed east to ask the Wrights for flying lessons. Johnstone, from Kansas City, Missouri, had gone into vaudeville as a trick cyclist. He did flips on his bicycle off a springboard—an act so risky that a friend suggested he do something safer. Johnstone thought it over and took up flying.

Hoxsey and Johnstone had made reams of newspaper copy by chasing each other around the sky in one air show after another. They were the hottest pilots the Wrights had—too hot, in fact, for Wilbur, who scolded them like a worried father for their recklessness. Not long before the Belmont Park meet, Wilbur had grounded Hoxsey temporarily for having "swooped and corkscrewed all over the place" in an air show at Detroit.

The Heavenly Twins' most memorable performance at Belmont Park was unplanned. Dueling one afternoon for an altitude record, they got into high winds that increased in strength until they found themselves

Picture Section, Part 1

The New York Times

Sunday, November 6 1910

actually being blown backward. Johnstone calculated his air speed at 40 miles per hour against a wind of 80 miles per hour. He managed to get his plane down in a clearing 55 miles from Belmont Park and tie it to a tree before it could blow away. Hoxsey, after a similarly wild ride to the rear, landed 25 miles away. It was, remarked Wilbur Wright appreciatively, "the first cross-country flight ever made tail end foremost."

The stunts that spiced the first seven days of flying at Belmont Park set up the crowd for the meet's main event, the race for the Gordon Bennett Cup. As usual, Grahame-White was the first to make his bid around the 20-lap course. The Frenchman Leblanc, whose protests against the treacherous course had been fruitless, followed in another Blériot, with a slightly shorter wingspan and a more sharply pitched propeller than Grahame-White's. At the 17th lap, Grahame-White's engine overheated, scorching his plane's fuselage. Smoke seared his throat and distorted his vision, but he completed the remaining three laps. He finished just as Leblanc, out of gas, went down on the backstretch, hanging his plane up on one of the telegraph poles he had complained about.

Walter Brookins, chief pilot of the Wright team, was readying the Baby Grand for its try when Leblanc crashed. Brookins flew over to

A picture page from The New York Times shows Claude Grahame-White (top) passing the Belmont Park stands at 60 mph to win the Gordon Bennett Cup. American John Moisant, pictured above with a frequent passenger he called Mademoiselle Paree, came in second.

England's champion, Claude Grahame-White, and the equally celebrated American actress Pauline Chase, close friends for seven years, enjoy a stroll during the air meet at New York's Belmont Park.

have a look and promptly wrecked his own plane. Pushed by a hefty tail wind, Brookins was going 100 miles per hour when one of his connecting rods broke.

"I tried to set her down as lightly as possible," he recalled, "but the light landing gear wouldn't stand the terrific speed." The Baby Grand's undercarriage crumpled and the craft began to cartwheel. "The first three or four somersaults were enough for me," said Brookins. "I got off then, and what was left of the ship turned a dozen or so more. I had started out to see what had happened to Leblanc and when they brought him into the hospital tent, there I was lying on the operating table waiting for him."

The two crashes injured neither pilot seriously, but with both the Baby Grand and Leblanc's fast Blériot out of the race Grahame-White's time of 61 minutes 4.74 seconds for the 100 kilometer distance stood untouched. Only three other pilots even finished the course; Moisant, who came in second, required almost an hour longer than Grahame-White, including 38 minutes on the ground for repairs.

The final event of the Belmont Park meet, a 33-mile race across the crowded city, then out over New York Harbor, around the Statue of Liberty and back, provided new cause for protest and for ill will. Originally, the race was open only to pilots who during the meet had completed a flight lasting at least one hour. But when it became apparent that very few aviators besides Grahame-White would meet that requirement, the judges abolished it, opening the race to everyone. Incensed, Grahame-White lodged a complaint and when the judges ignored him, he considered withdrawing from the race.

Even the rule change failed to provide enough aviators for a sporting contest. The race was scheduled for a Sunday; the devout Wright brothers never flew on the Sabbath, and neither did their team. John Moisant was scratched early, or so it seemed, when he wrecked his Blériot in a runway collision with Clifford Harmon's clumsy Farman. Only the Blériot team's Count Jacques de Lesseps (a grandson of the Suez Canal builder) remained. Then, at the last minute, Grahame-White had a change of heart. Spurred perhaps by the realization that his plane far outpowered de Lesseps', he decided to stay in the race.

Between the two Blériots, there was little contest. De Lesseps took off first, but Grahame-White soon passed him and held a 65-second lead by the time he reached the balloon tethered over the statue, marking the turn. As boat whistles shrilled in the harbor, Grahame-White banked around the statue, headed back across Brooklyn and landed. He was being paraded around the race track, wrapped in a Union Jack, when it was announced by megaphone that the competition was not yet over. John Moisant had appeared at the starting line in a new Blériot. It was 4:06 p.m.—21 minutes after the official closing time for the race. The judges again had bent the rules.

Moisant, after mangling his own machine in the runway accident, had refused to call it quits. He and his banker brother Alfred had spotted a spare Blériot in the injured Alfred Leblanc's hangar and decided, impulsively, that they would buy it. While John Moisant supervised a quick switch of identification numbers on the plane's wing and tail, Alfred Moisant got on the telephone to Leblanc in his Manhattan hotel room to negotiate the purchase.

Leblanc recovered sufficiently to find a car and drive to Belmont Park to meet with the brothers. They haggled over price; Alfred Moisant, growing impatient, offered $10,000, far more than the Blériot was worth. Leblanc accepted on the spot.

Alfred, who was without his checkbook, borrowed a check from a bystander and clinched the deal. Within 10 minutes, the paint on the new numbers still wet, John Moisant taxied to the starting line and took off. As the Blériot melted from view, Belmont Park buzzed with anticipation. An American still had a chance for the prize.

In less than a half hour, the lone airplane appeared again and landed amid the roar of the crowd. The judges deliberated, then made their announcement. By 43 seconds, Moisant was the winner.

John Moisant, flying his newly purchased Blériot, rounds the Statue of Liberty in the final race of the Belmont Park meet. Although Moisant had started after the deadline, he was declared the winner—a decision that was later reversed.

The victory was tainted but the crowd went wild. Even Wilbur Wright lost his starchy dignity and was seen "dancing on his hat and whooping like a Comanche Indian," as one British writer put it. Moisant was paraded in triumph around the field, wearing an American flag draped over his shoulders like a Salvadoran serape.

Grahame-White was furious. He demanded a rerun, fired off a scorching cable of protest to the Fédération Aéronautique Internationale in Paris, then offered to race Moisant anywhere for a stake of $10,000. Moisant refused. "Really, this man is absolutely the sorest loser I have ever met," he said. "I have beaten him once in an inferior machine. Why should I risk my neck to beat him again?"

It was more than a year before the dispute was settled. Then the F.A.I., meeting in Rome, reversed the judges' decision, and at an Aero Club dinner in New York in 1912, Grahame-White finally collected his $10,000 check—plus $500 accrued interest.

By then John Moisant was dead. So were two other popular heroes of the Belmont Park meet: Arch Hoxsey and Ralph Johnstone.

Moisant was killed in New Orleans on December 31, 1910, while trying to squeeze out a victory—on the last possible day of competition—in the Michelin tire company's annual 20,000-franc ($4,000) contest for the longest sustained flight of the calendar year. Moisant's Blériot went into a nose dive—apparently after its heavy gasoline load shifted forward; no one was ever sure.

Hoxsey was killed the same day in Los Angeles while trying to beat his own world's altitude record of 11,474 feet, set five days previously. Flying in high winds, he had spun in from 7,000 feet. Hoxsey's flying partner, Ralph Johnstone, had died less than three weeks after the meet at Belmont Park. As the New York *Tribune* reported, Johnstone was attempting to give the spectators at Denver's Overland Park an extra thrill with his most daring feat, the spiral glide, when the tips of both his wings "folded up as though they had been hinged."

Johnstone rode the crippled plane down from 800 feet, pulling at the warping wires with his hands in a futile effort to right it. Spectators who scattered in terror as the plane fell rushed back to paw the wreckage for bloodied pieces of wood and to snatch Johnstone's gloves from his dead hands.

Surviving Johnstone were some bitter words he had written for the *Cleveland Plain Dealer* not long before his last flight: "I fly to live. If I didn't have to, I wouldn't. I am a fatalist. I believe that every man's time is marked out for him, only those of us who are drawn for the air game have their time black-inked well up toward the head of the list. The only way to cheat it is to quit. But if you're marked down to stay, then you can't quit until it gets you. Let me tell you, the people who go to see us want thrills. And, if we fall, do they think of us and go away weeping? Not by a long shot. They're too busy watching the next man and wondering if he will repeat the performance."

Pacesetters of an era

They were benchmarks of progress—a dozen planes that, among all others, had the greatest impact on the first decade of the air age. Aside from the Wright Flyer III *(below)*, which stands alone as history's first practical airplane, they are presented here and on the following pages in approximate scale to one another, along with the names of their designers and the years when they were built.

Some of the planes, like the Wright Flyer and Louis Blériot's Model XI *(page 111)*, set standards of achievement for others to match, and some represented breakthroughs in technology and design. Almost every plane was carried from concept to completion by one or two individuals supported only by a small team. Together these craft illustrate how, in a very few years, airplanes began to evolve from little more than fragile, winged frames into sleek, fully enclosed, passenger-carrying ships that hinted strongly of shapes to come.

WRIGHT FLYER III—WRIGHT BROTHERS (1905)
Capable of flying for 38 minutes on its modest fuel supply, Flyer III had skids for landing gear, a forward elevator and a 20-hp engine that could push it at 35 mph.

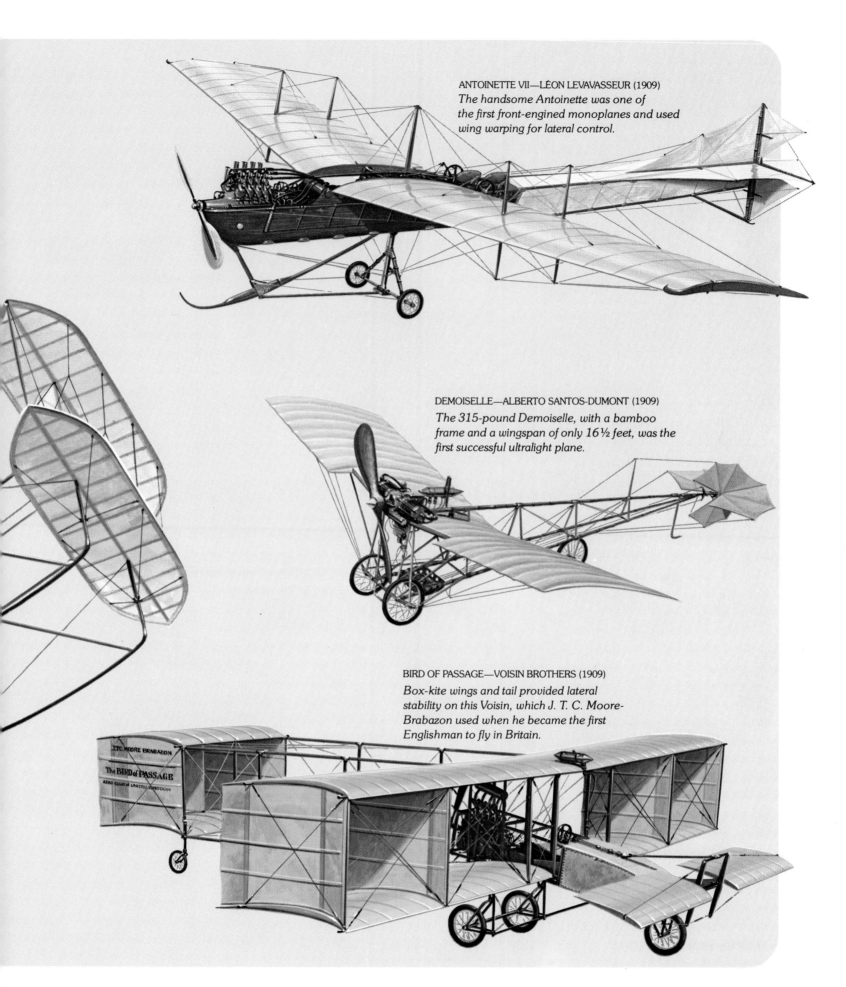

ANTOINETTE VII—LÉON LEVAVASSEUR (1909)

The handsome Antoinette was one of the first front-engined monoplanes and used wing warping for lateral control.

DEMOISELLE—ALBERTO SANTOS-DUMONT (1909)

The 315-pound Demoiselle, with a bamboo frame and a wingspan of only 16½ feet, was the first successful ultralight plane.

BIRD OF PASSAGE—VOISIN BROTHERS (1909)

Box-kite wings and tail provided lateral stability on this Voisin, which J. T. C. Moore-Brabazon used when he became the first Englishman to fly in Britain.

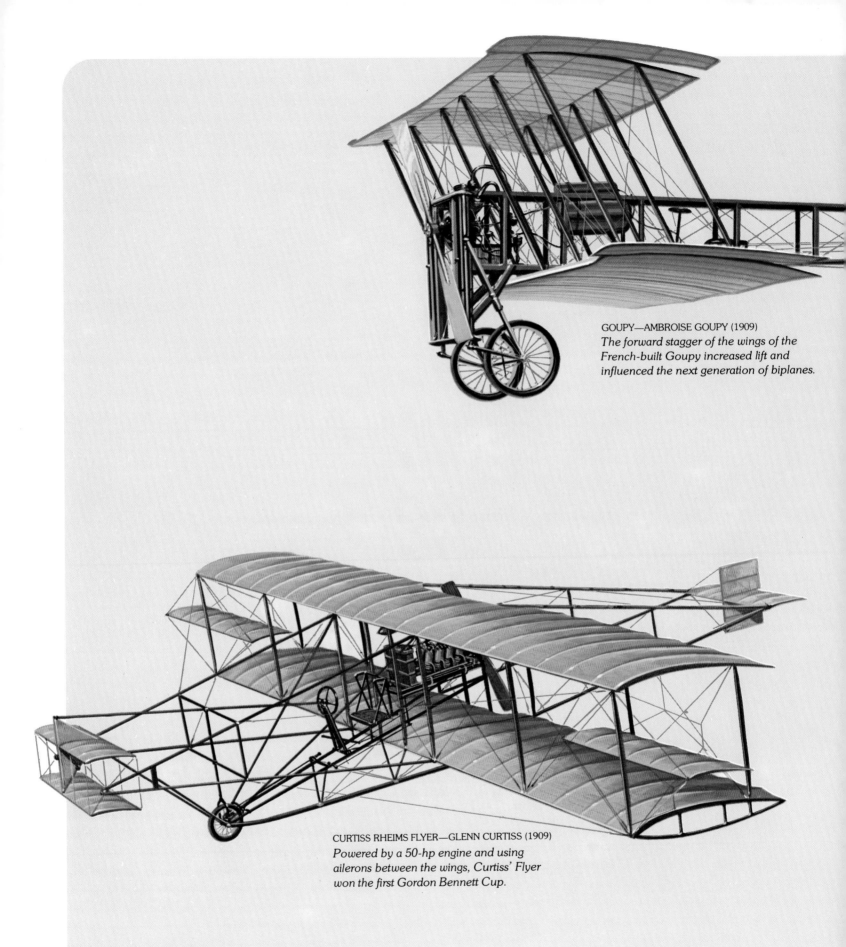

GOUPY—AMBROISE GOUPY (1909)
The forward stagger of the wings of the French-built Goupy increased lift and influenced the next generation of biplanes.

CURTISS RHEIMS FLYER—GLENN CURTISS (1909)
Powered by a 50-hp engine and using ailerons between the wings, Curtiss' Flyer won the first Gordon Bennett Cup.

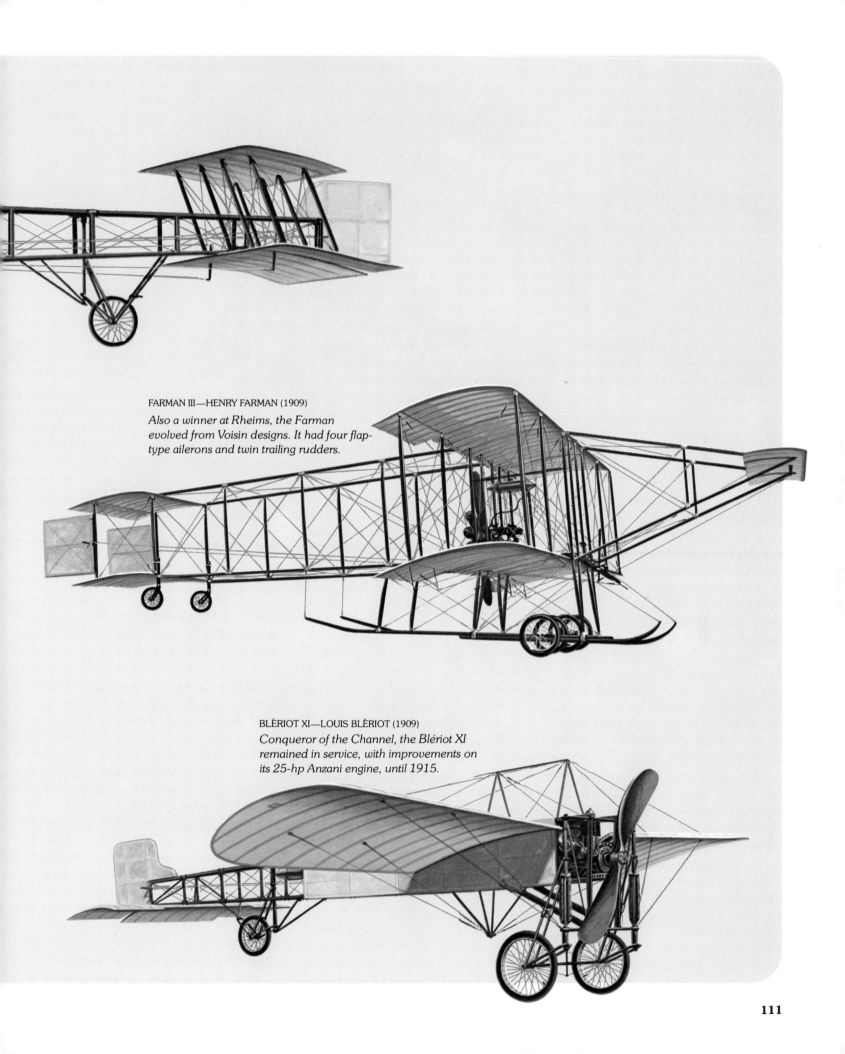

FARMAN III—HENRY FARMAN (1909)

Also a winner at Rheims, the Farman evolved from Voisin designs. It had four flap-type ailerons and twin trailing rudders.

BLÉRIOT XI—LOUIS BLÉRIOT (1909)

Conqueror of the Channel, the Blériot XI remained in service, with improvements on its 25-hp Anzani engine, until 1915.

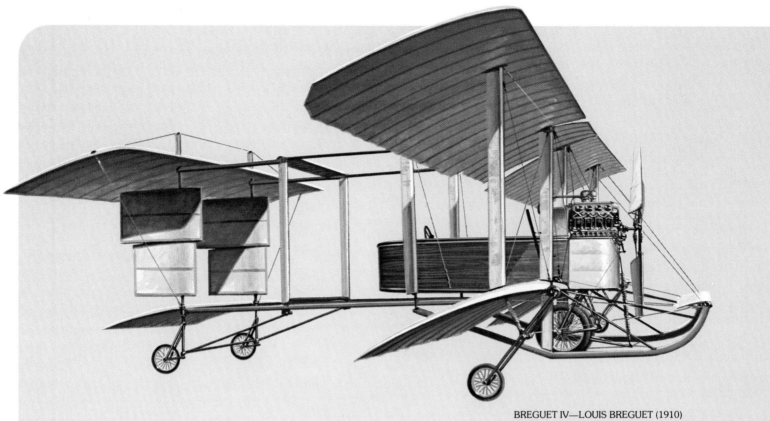

BREGUET IV—LOUIS BREGUET (1910)
Ancestor of the airliner, the Breguet IV was designed to carry six passengers seated in front of the pilot in its open cockpit.

AVRO F—A. V. ROE (1912)
The first enclosed-cabin monoplane, the Avro had a tube-steel frame, skin of linen and aluminum, and celluloid windows.

NIEUPORT IV G—ÉDOUARD NIEUPORT (1911)
Advancing the basic Blériot design a step, Nieuport created a plane with a fully enclosed, streamlined fuselage. It set a world speed record of 82.73 mph.

DEPERDUSSIN RACER—LOUIS BÉCHEREAU (1913)
French engineer Béchereau produced the first monocoque fuselage, which used the plane's entire body shell, rather than just the frame, to carry the load.

4

The Wrights vs. the world

One day in March 1910, the visiting French aviator Louis Paulhan was working in a rented hangar at Jamaica race track in New York City when Wilbur Wright stalked in. Flanking Wilbur were a pair of lawyers, a clear sign that this was no social visit. Paulhan, for his part, harbored no fondness for Wilbur or his brother Orville. Paulhan had been in the midst of a lucrative American exhibition tour when the Wrights got an injunction against him, charging that his imported airplanes—two Farmans and two Blériots—infringed on Wright patents. Paulhan could continue flying for profit only if he posted a $25,000 bond, and this he refused to do.

Paulhan made an effort to be civil as Wilbur approached. "He was under my roof," the Frenchman explained. "I welcomed him, I shook his hand." But Wilbur was not mollified. "He hardly answered me," Paulhan recalled. "Instead he threw himself on our machines, touching everything, shouting and yelling like a madman. With those lawyers, he put me through a veritable inquisition, questioning my good faith. He is, I tell you, a man of prey."

In Wilbur's view, the situation was just the reverse: He and Orville were the ones being preyed upon. "We made the art of flying possible, and all the people in it have us to thank," Wilbur had said. "In 1900 the probability that any man would get back any part of the money he invested in flying experiments was not valued at one chance in a million," he declared. "Yet on such a chance we spent every cent we had accumulated by years of saving, and we worked night and day for years amid the laughter of the world. We have never taken any legal action against any man unless he wantonly tried to make money for himself by pirating our particular inventions without compensation to us."

Tragically, as the lawsuits proliferated—first against the hated Glenn Curtiss, then against Paulhan, Grahame-White, Farman and others who flew for profit—it was the Wrights themselves who were most harmed. The interminable court proceedings drained their creative energy, left them frustrated and bitter and cost them the leadership of a science they had largely created. Just seven years after their historic first flight, and barely two years after they astonished Europe with their mastery of the air and came home to belated homage in their own country, the Wrights were in eclipse.

Against Curtiss, the Wrights had won the first round of legal skirmishing. In January 1910, Federal Judge John R. Hazel declared that the

Unsmiling even in success, Orville and Wilbur Wright and sister Katharine return from a triumphal tour of Europe in 1909. Soon they became embroiled in legal action against rival plane builders, charging infringement of their patents—an obsession that came to dominate their lives.

Wright patent claims covered virtually any device then in use to control the stability of an airplane. It was a ruling with far-reaching implications for the nascent airplane industry, but it did not stand for long. In June, an appellate court overruled Judge Hazel; the Wrights again challenged, and the prolonged struggle against Curtiss—"for revenge and prestige," as a Wright partisan described it—was on in earnest.

The contest assumed the proportions of a blood feud that embraced the entire Wright camp, where Curtiss was regarded not as an inventor or engineer but as a devious self-promoter who had been stealing the Wrights' ideas since 1908. "We were taught that the Curtiss crowd was just no good at all," said Frank Coffyn of the Wright exhibition team.

The Wrights' bitterness also showed in the highly technical depositions that piled up during years of legal wrangling. They projected themselves in court as "persons skilled in the art," who were protecting their brain child from an upstart competitor with little experience and less scientific ability. In response to one Curtiss affidavit, the Wrights replied that "Mr. Curtiss shows his incompetence to give expert testimony as to what actually occurs on his machine, and even seems to raise a direct question of veracity."

Curtiss, for his part, tried several times to negotiate a settlement with the Wrights out of court; each time, the brothers spurned his overtures. Angrily, he refuted their accusations of piracy as "absurd if not malicious." As he well knew, a Wright victory in court could spell the end of his business, which would be hard pressed to survive the heavy payments in royalties the Wrights would impose. So he stood his ground.

However justified the Wrights might have been, their legal assaults "turned the hand of almost *every* man in aviation against them," as even their loyal associate Grover Loening later conceded. Editorialists lambasted the brothers as selfish monopolizers. They were caricatured mercilessly in newspaper cartoons, one of which depicted them as pointing aloft and shouting: "Keep out of my air!" Moreover, their campaign marred their long and cherished friendship with their staunchest supporter, Octave Chanute. After the Wrights sued Glenn Curtiss, Chanute suggested publicly that they were making a grave mistake. Privately, he sent Wilbur a stinging rebuke: "I am afraid, my friend, that your usually sound judgment has been warped by the desire for great wealth."

Such an accusation from a devoted friend cut the Wright brothers deeply. Wilbur replied: "You apparently concede to us no right to compensation for the solution of a problem ages old. We honestly think that our work of 1900-1906 has been and will be of value to the world, and that the world owes us something as inventors." Great wealth had never been their goal, Wilbur protested, but rather mere financial freedom—"sufficient compensation to enable us to live modestly with enough surplus income to permit the devotion of our future time to scientific experimenting instead of business."

Jules Védrines, a former chauffeur and the son of working-class Parisians, flew over the Pyrenees in the 1911 Paris-Madrid race, becoming the only pilot to finish.

French Navy lieutenant Jean Conneau, a skilled navigator at sea, used a compass, roller maps and other such aids to win the three major European air races of 1911.

There would be precious little time, or energy, for experimenting. Long before the courts—and outside events—ended the patent fight, the brothers had been worn down under the excruciating press of legal and business concerns. As they fought to exact their reward for past labors, they virtually ceased to look ahead. New designs that might have kept them in the vanguard of aviation were not forthcoming. The Belmont Park meet of 1910 was the last at which a Wright-built plane presented a threat to the rapidly improving European machines.

It was not only the Wrights who were being outclassed; except in the development of seaplanes, where Glenn Curtiss was beginning to emerge as a leader, the brief American supremacy in aviation was over. By 1911, European planes had become measurably superior both in design and performance. And of them all, the planes made in France were the most advanced.

At the end of 1911, the world's altitude record of 12,828 feet was held by a Blériot XI, flown by Frenchman Roland Garros. The records for both speed (82.73 miles per hour) and endurance (460 miles) belonged to a streamlined monoplane with a fully enclosed fuselage recently developed by Édouard Nieuport, a French electrical engineer.

French mastery of the skies was emphasized even more dramatically that year in a series of long-distance races that galvanized the Continent. The great capitals of Western Europe served as pylons for these marathons, which included races from Paris to Madrid and from Paris to Rome, circuits of several cities within Great Britain, Germany and Italy—and even a three-nation Circuit of Europe.

No American-made planes were entered in these events, and perhaps it was just as well. The French entries—Blériots, Deperdussins, Nieuports and others—thoroughly outclassed the competition. The four biggest events were dominated by three pilots, all French: Jean Conneau, a Navy lieutenant on extended leave who flew under a civilian nom de plume as André Beaumont; Jules Védrines, a terrible-tempered ex-factory worker from the back streets of Paris; and the suave veteran Roland Garros, who was just back from a tour of the United States, Mexico and Cuba.

Conneau, an expert navigator, entered his races meticulously prepared. The tiny cockpit of his Blériot XI was crammed full of instruments, including compass, clock, altimeter, and a handy new contrivance, a map on rollers that could be unraveled as the journey progressed. In contrast, Védrines flew by the seat of his pants, scorning even a compass. "I don't understand anything about that gadget," he said. "It always turns like crazy when I look at it."

The first important race of 1911, from Paris to Madrid, began tragically on a Sunday in May when an overflow throng of 300,000 spectators forced a party of official visitors out onto the runway—directly into the path of an airplane that was trying to take off. The plane struck the officials; the Premier of France, Ernest Monis, was seriously injured, and the Minister of War, Maurice Berteaux, was killed outright.

After a token postponement of one day, the race went on. Conneau, for all his preparation, cracked up on the very first leg while Védrines and Garros forged ahead. Over the Pyrenees, Védrines fought off a marauding eagle and, near San Sebastian, left Garros behind with engine trouble. Alone now in the race, Védrines soared southward to land at Madrid; his flying time, spread over three days, had been 14 hours 55 minutes. But the expected crowd had gone home, and Védrines, tired and disappointed, flew into a rage—even making "some dirty remarks," it was reported, about Spain's King Alfonso XIII. The King, apparently willing to forgive anything in an aviator, overlooked Védrines' surliness and invited him to the bullfights.

By the following week, Védrines was enjoying himself so thoroughly in Madrid that he missed the start of the next big race, from Paris to Rome. In that contest Conneau and Garros battled neck and neck for the lead. Conneau's precise navigation—and the fact that Garros twice had to change planes en route after smashing up on landing—enabled him to beat Garros into Rome by a full day. Conneau received a welcome that would have satisfied even Védrines. The Pope blessed his Blériot as it flew past the Vatican, and Roman crowds went into a frenzy as he landed.

The first Circuit of Europe, in June, got off to a grisly start when three pilots were killed in crashes on the first day. Conneau once again outraced his rivals over the exacting course, which required nine flights spread over 13 days, from Paris through France and Belgium, then across the Channel to England and back. Fifty-two planes entered the race and nine finished.

The Circuit of Britain, in July, turned into a duel between Conneau and Védrines. Plagued by airsickness over Scotland's craggy Highlands, Védrines lost his way several times on the home stretch to London. He nevertheless finished second to the methodical Conneau, who pocketed the entire £10,000 purse; Védrines scowlingly accepted £200 that had been raised at the last minute as a consolation prize.

Conneau's victories in three of the most demanding aerial events of the year made him the toast of Europe. Capitalizing on his fame, he published *My Three Big Flights,* a book that sold wildly and added handsomely to the $126,000 prize money he had won in the races. In the book, Conneau persuasively argued the importance of navigation in flying. Thanks in large part to his influence, compasses began to appear with frequency in the cockpits of airplanes, and aviators were awakened to the possibilities of other instruments that would, in time, become as vital to them as their own eyes.

The European flying season of 1911 had been a sequence of long-distance adventures, but the longest pilgrimage of the year was attempted not in Europe but in the United States. It was no triumph of technology; the machine involved literally had to be replaced, piece by broken

Linked by a desire to promote progress in aviation, allegorical figures representing France and Italy join their hands in a magazine illustration on the eve of the Paris-to-Rome air race in 1911.

Jean Conneau, on the way to winning the 1911 Paris-Rome race, evokes a blessing from Pope Pius X as his Blériot monoplane appears over the dome of St. Peter's in this contemporary painting.

piece, as the journey progressed. But as a test of perseverance, it was a flight unprecedented in the short history of aviation.

The incentive was a $50,000 prize for the first coast-to-coast crossing of the United States within a 30-day period. The contest, announced the year before by newspaper publisher William Randolph Hearst, had an expiration date of October 10, 1911. Not until a month before the deadline did anyone take off in pursuit of the prize.

Then, on September 11, 1911, a novice Wright pilot named Robert Fowler started eastward from San Francisco; he circled over the Golden Gate and reached Sacramento, 85 miles away, before landing for the first time. Ahead of him lay the challenging High Sierra. Two days later an ex-jockey from Chicago, James J. Ward, flying a Curtiss machine, headed west out of New York—only to lose his way over the New Jersey railroad yards and come down just 20 miles away. While Fowler and Ward struggled onward, a third contestant entered the race, flying a Wright EX (for experimental) biplane. He was a jovial, nearly deaf giant of a man named Calbraith Perry Rodgers.

The Wrights, who had built the Model EX especially for Rodgers, had some misgivings about their machine, a smaller, single-seated version of their Model B, equipped with both skids and wheels and with a top speed of 60 miles per hour. But they had full confidence in the pilot. Then 32 years old, Rodgers stood six feet four inches tall and weighed 192 pounds. He would have become a naval officer had not a child-hood attack of scarlet fever severely impaired his hearing. He came from a line of American naval heroes that included Commodore Oliver Hazard Perry, who had won the battle of Lake Erie in the War of 1812, and Commodore Matthew Calbraith Perry, who had led the naval squadron that opened Japan to the West in 1854.

Unable to get into Annapolis, Rodgers enrolled at Columbia, where he played football and raced yachts and cars before taking up flying. At the Wright school in 1911 he soloed after 90 minutes of instruction—a record for the school. Two months later, at an international air meet in Chicago, Rodgers took aim at the prize for durability. "I looked over the prize list," he said, "picked the biggest one on it and determined to bend all my energies toward winning it." He won $11,285 by logging 27 hours in the air, more than anyone else at the nine-day meet. Then he turned his sights on the $50,000 transcontinental.

In return for free advertising, the Armour Company of Chicago, one of whose products was a soft drink known as Vin Fiz, agreed to pay Rodgers five dollars for every mile he flew. In addition, the company paid for a special train to follow him, with a Pullman car and day coach for his wife, mother, mechanics and other helpers, and a third "hangar car" that carried a spare airplane, $4,000 worth of parts, gasoline and oil. Armour also contributed a truck that could be used to transport Rodgers' plane on the ground and a Palmer-Singer racing car for getting to Rodgers himself in a hurry, with medical aid, in case he needed it.

In late afternoon on Sunday, September 17, 1911, Rodgers climbed

Ground crewmen await a pilot's signal to release his Deperdussin monoplane for takeoff from Calais in the 1911 Circuit of Europe.

into the *Vin Fiz Flyer,* as he had named his Wright plane, and took off from a race track near Sheepshead Bay, New York. The first leg of his trip went like a charm. Rodgers lit up a cigar and followed white canvas strips laid at intervals along the Erie Railroad tracks. In less than two hours he had reached Middletown, New York, 84 miles northwest, landing so easily, he said, "it didn't knock the ashes off my cigar. It's Chicago in four days," he added, "if everything goes right."

Everything did not. As Rodgers took off the next day he clipped a tree and had time for just one thought—"Oh, my beautiful plane!"—before crashing into a nearby backyard, nose down in a chicken coop. His temple was badly gashed but he still had his cigar. The Wright brothers' longtime mechanic, Charlie Taylor, on loan to Rodgers for the trip, supervised the rebuilding of the plane. Rodgers broke a skid on the next lap during a mushy landing in a potato field after a defective spark plug popped out of the cylinder head. The next day, after taking a wrong turn at a railroad junction and wandering south into Pennsylvania, Rodgers landed at Scranton and almost lost his machine to souvenir hunters; he caught one man trying to chisel off a valve.

By week's end he was a long way from Chicago but had nearly crossed New York State, sometimes flying with one hand while holding a loose spark plug in place with the other. Then, on takeoff from the Allegheny Indian Reservation 60 miles south of Buffalo, he snagged a barbed wire fence and smashed his plane for a second time.

By now Rodgers was alone in the race. Out in the Sierra, Fowler had

An appreciative crowd greets Jean Conneau of France as he lands at Brooklands outside London to win the Circuit of Britain in July 1911. His rival, Jules Védrines, flying with no instruments, had lost his way in the unfamiliar Scottish Highlands.

wrestled his Wright up to 8,000 feet over the Donner Pass, but his radiator boiled over and he was forced to turn back; he shipped the plane to Los Angeles for a later try via a more southerly route. (He finally made it across country to Jacksonville, Florida, in February 1912.) The other competitor, James Ward, had done no better. "Who in the world would think that the oiling system of a new $2,000 Curtiss motor would go wrong during the first hour of its flight?" he moaned, after a breakdown in Corning, New York. Gamblers were betting 5 to 1 that Ward would be killed before he reached Buffalo. The gamblers almost collected; on September 22, Ward flipped over while landing at Addison, New York, and his wife and manager prevailed on him to abandon the flight.

Rodgers, his plane repaired, slogged resolutely westward. Dexterous piloting got him past a drenching thunderstorm over eastern Indiana: "First thing I knew I was riding through an electric gridiron," he reported. "I seemed to have run into a cloud convention. I took off my gloves and covered what I could of the vital points of the magneto. It was a cold and painful situation. The earth had disappeared. I might be a million miles up in space. I might be a hundred feet from earth." The storm passed, and Rodgers caught up with his train at Huntington, Indiana. The next day, trying to avoid a crowd of spectators, he crashed again on takeoff. Again, the *Vin Fiz Flyer* had to be rebuilt.

By the time Rodgers touched down in Chicago on October 8, only two days remained before the $50,000 Hearst offer expired, and he still had two thirds of the country to cross. Nevertheless, he declared his determination to reach California: "Prize or no prize, that's where I am bound, and if canvas, steel and wire—together with a little brawn, tendon and brain—stick with me, I mean to get there."

Heading southwest across Missouri, Kansas and Oklahoma, Rodgers enlivened his hours aloft by racing express trains. On reaching Fort Worth, Texas, he amused himself by flying figure 8s between two water towers on a military base. He made it to Spofford, Texas, before his next major crack-up; on taking off, he hit a stump and demolished his airplane. Patched up and en route again with a new engine, he was cruising at 4,000 feet over the Salton Sea, in Southern California, when a cylinder blew out, tearing the engine apart and driving steel shards into his arm. The plane went into a dive, but Rodgers pulled it out and landed safely at the town of Imperial Junction for repairs to man and machine. Doctors removed the metal splinters; mechanics removed the engine and installed the original one, which Taylor had overhauled.

More trouble followed at San Gorgonio Pass, near the desert settlement of Palm Springs, where Rodgers had to cope with treacherous air currents and a magneto that threatened to break loose. The next day, Sunday, November 5, 1911, he flew 81 miles and reached Pasadena, landing beside a sheet staked out in Tournament Park, site of the city's annual Tournament of Roses. He had flown 4,231 miles; the Pacific Ocean was only 20 miles farther. As far as the newspapers were concerned, he had completed his trip. But the following Sunday he set out

A poster distributed by his sponsor, a soda-pop manufacturer, traces Calbraith Rodgers' 1911 transcontinental marathon and lists the painful statistics.

to fly the remaining distance to the water's edge. At Compton, still 12 miles short, the reconditioned engine failed and Rodgers came down hard in a plowed field. The concussion knocked him unconscious, he suffered internal injuries and one of his ankles was broken.

"It's all in the ball game," he announced from his hospital bed. "I am going to finish that flight." Four weeks later, with his crutches strapped to his plane's wing, Rodgers did just that. On December 10 he flew on to Long Beach, landed on the sand and wet his wheels in the surf.

Rodgers' odyssey was over. America had been crossed, and though it had taken 84 days, Rodgers had averaged almost a mile a minute while he was aloft. He had endured five major crashes, numerous lesser mishaps on takeoff or landing, engine failures in mid-air and a hospital stay. Of his original plane, only the rudder and the oil drip pan remained; everything else had been replaced at least once.

For all his exertions, without the Hearst prize Rodgers had made little profit from his historic flight. Repairs had consumed the Vin Fiz subsidy; to earn money along the way, his wife had set herself up as postmistress of the "Rodgers Aerial Post," offering people the chance, for 25 cents, to have a postcard carried in Rodgers' plane to his next stopping place, where the regular postal service would forward it to its destination.

The following spring, Rodgers made a final visit to the spot where he had ended his trip. In an exhibition flight on April 3, 1912, he buzzed the amusement park at Long Beach and then headed exuberantly out over the waves, to the delight of the 7,000 spectators below. Reported *The New York Herald:* "Seeing a flock of gulls disporting themselves among a great shoal of sardines just over the breakers, Rodgers again turned and dived down into them, scattering the seafowl in all directions." One gull, however, became wedged between the rudder and the tail of the plane, breaking the control wire; it was jammed so tightly that the rudder had to be broken to pull the bird loose, after the wreckage of the plane, and Rodgers' body, were recovered from the water.

Rodgers' flight had demonstrated that airplanes were not yet as tough as the men who flew them. Four fitting words were carved on his tombstone in Pittsburgh, Pennsylvania: "I Endure—I Conquer."

In the same season as Calbraith Rodgers' peregrination, Orville Wright managed to slip his leash as supervising engineer for the Wright Company and make his way to Kitty Hawk. There he planned glider tests of an automatic stabilizer he had been working on since 1907; it was a device that activated the wing-warping system of an airplane to counteract unintentional roll and moved the elevators to control pitch, thus keeping the craft on an even keel without help from the pilot.

When the press appeared at Kitty Hawk, Orville, secretive as ever, decided not to test the stabilizer. But he made the most of his three-week sojourn among the familiar dunes, setting a gliding record on October 24 of 9 minutes 45 seconds—a mark that stood for a decade. By 1913 he had perfected and patented the automatic stabilizer, which won him the Collier Trophy for aerial achievement. That same year he tackled the problem of stalling in mid-air and produced an angle-of-incidence indicator that showed pilots when their planes were climbing too steeply, thus helping them avoid stalls before they occurred.

Wilbur Wright's contributions to aviation had ended earlier. By mid-1910 he had almost entirely given up piloting. Once he had been meticulous about keeping in flying trim, practicing the controls by the hour in the hangar. Now he was completely absorbed in the patent fight, in money squabbles with air-show promoters ("the Belmont swindlers are still trying to unload the results of their own incompetence on us") and in trying to improve the poor profit performance of the Wright companies abroad ("more the result of bad management than rascality, though the latter may not be entirely lacking").

By early 1912, Wilbur was spending weeks on end in court, where he made a masterful witness; attorneys for Curtiss conceded that much. But in May he returned home from a business trip to Boston with a high fever, diagnosed first as a minor indisposition, then as typhoid. As the fever rose, Wilbur rallied his strength for one last letter railing at the law's delays, which, he said, "have already destroyed fully three fourths of the value of our patent." He added:

"Innumerable competitors are entering the field, and for the first time are producing machines which will really fly. These machines are being put on the market at one half less than the price which we have been selling our machines for. Up to the present time a decision in our favor would have given us a monopoly, but if we wait too long a favorable decision may have little value to us."

Less than a month later, Wilbur was dead. On Thursday, May 30, 1912, the aged Bishop Wright recorded the end in his diary: "This morning at 3:15, Wilbur passed away, aged 45 years, 1 month and 14 days. A short life, full of consequences. An unfailing intellect, imperturbable temper, great self-reliance and as great modesty, seeing the right clearly, pursuing it steadily, he lived and died. Many called—many telegrams (probably over a thousand)."

Wilbur's death released an outpouring of bitterness from his family. At the funeral, Katharine Wright was heard to remark: "I suppose the Curtiss crowd will be glad now Wilbur is gone." Orville clearly blamed Curtiss' legal maneuvering for the loss of his brother. "The delays were what worried him," he told a reporter, "first into a state of chronic nervousness, then into a physical fatigue which made him an easy prey for the attack of typhoid that caused his death."

The patent war did not end with Wilbur's life. Even after it had dragged to a weary conclusion, years later, a residue of ill will smoldered, and occasionally flared, as long as the remaining principals lived.

Orville Wright assumed the presidency of the Wright Company after Wilbur died, but without his brother he had little taste for the business. He grew distant and indecisive. The lingering effects of the injuries he had suffered in the Fort Myer crash in 1908 kept him in pain—a condition he attempted to hide. During the day he stayed away from the Wright factory, holing up instead in an office two miles away. He talked interminably with his sister, Katharine, of his grudge against Curtiss, and he shared his feelings at times with his young friend, the Wright Company engineer Grover Loening.

"As the months went by I learned that he was indeed a great genius but a troubled one," Loening observed. "He brooded much on the injustice of the rising competition that was robbing him of the fruits of invention. On this subject he would talk for hours."

Despite his concern about the competition, Orville did little to keep abreast of new developments in the field. The Europeans were turning out the designs that would shape the airplane of the future, but Orville seemed satisfied with his tried-and-true model, the pusher biplane, a type that was sliding swiftly toward obsolescence. He dismissed the new Continental designs as wrongheaded.

"An interesting angle of his thinking was revealed one day," said Loening, "when a discussion was held on the then-new vogue of the tractor types, with engine and propeller in front. Orville said, 'This type is really an invention of the French, and we should not be copying it just to keep up. There must be better reasons than that.' He picked up some foreign magazines and glanced at them. 'Since the chief use of airplanes for the military will be observation,' he continued, 'how can you justify putting the pilot behind so much engine-propeller interference, spoiling his view?' Having convinced himself, he threw the magazines down on the table."

The only thing that seemed to cheer Orville was flight itself. When he went aloft his depression faded and he recaptured the zest of the old days with Wilbur. "Whenever an occasion rose involving a flight test," Loening said, "Orville was a different man—keen, quick, careful and obviously one with the machine. There was no indecision then, no hesitating, no procrastinating. The master was on the job!"

In January 1914, Orville won what appeared to be total victory: A United States Circuit Court of Appeals judgment recognized him and Wilbur as "pioneers in the practical art of flying heavier-than-air machines" and ruled that their patent claims covered the use of ailerons as well as wing warping. Curtiss was permanently enjoined from the manufacture or sale of airplanes with ailerons operating simultaneously to produce differing angles on the wing tips. The Wright Company immediately announced its royalty terms: 20 per cent on every airplane sold in America. Orville, who disagreed with the company's Wall Street backers on how tight a monopoly to establish, indicated that he would apply "a policy of leniency" for most manufacturers. But not for Glenn Curtiss.

Curtiss rushed home from a European sales trip to face the disaster. He was not long in implementing a new set of tactics that rekindled the Curtiss-Wright feud—with some new characters in the drama. One was

Charles Walcott, the successor to aerial experimenter Samuel P. Langley as Secretary of the Smithsonian Institution in Washington. Another was the successful Detroit automobile maker Henry Ford.

Ford was a veteran of a patent war in his own industry. The stubborn production genius had been the only manufacturer bold enough to buck a 1909 court ruling that set up a monopoly for the holders of a patent on an engine for a horseless carriage, originally applied for in 1879 by an inventor named George Selden. Ford alone had refused to pay the royalties demanded of every automobile company; instead, he went to court and in 1911 broke the Selden strangle hold.

In 1913, according to published accounts, Ford chanced on Glenn Curtiss in the dining room of New York's Brevoort Hotel. "Well, I see they have you with your back nearly to the wall," Ford was quoted as telling Curtiss. "When they get you right up against it, come to see me."

Whether or not the conversation actually took place, Curtiss did contact Ford in early 1914, after the Wright patent had been upheld, and soon a publicity-wise patent lawyer, W. Benton Crisp—who had been Ford's attorney in the Selden case—took over as Curtiss' legal strategist. The sharp-eyed Crisp quickly spotted a loophole in the Wright patent ruling. The patent, the court had written, covered the use of ailerons that operated *simultaneously*—on the inadvertent use of this word hinged Crisp's scheme. At his advice, Curtiss devised and then announced a new control system that allowed the aileron on one wing to move up and down independently of the aileron on the opposite wing. An interlock prevented their simultaneous operation. The Wright Company promptly sued again, and the patent war resumed.

Meanwhile, there had been some curious proceedings at the Smithsonian Institution involving the Langley Aerodrome, a tandem-winged craft that twice had plunged into the Potomac River on launching in the autumn of 1903, shortly before the Wrights' first powered flight at Kitty Hawk. Langley had died in 1906 without trying again. On the authority of Secretary Walcott, the old Aerodrome was taken out of storage in April of 1914 and shipped to the Curtiss factory at Hammondsport, New York—where, for a fee of $2,000, Curtiss intended to rehabilitate the machine and try to fly it.

As a research project, the Smithsonian's posthumous rescue of "Langley's Folly," as the $70,000 failure had been called, was legitimate enough. But the timing of the venture and the choice of people to carry it out cast doubt on the Institution's motives.

With the Wright-Curtiss legal fight still unresolved, the impact that a flight by the Langley machine might have was obvious. The Wrights had been granted patents because their machine was the first to fly. If it could be demonstrated that another machine was capable of flight before the Wright Flyer, those patents would be in grave danger.

Secretary Walcott's selection of Curtiss—hardly an unbiased party—to rebuild and fly the Aerodrome aroused suspicions. So did the

A wonderful array of odd birds

The early years of aviation produced scores of quixotic craft that lifted some eyebrows but little else. Their often radical designs were inspired in part by a need to differ from the Wright brothers, whose patents tended to block others from using the Wrights' basic configuration.

Some of the odd birds flew, or at least hopped. In 1904 Britain's Horatio Phillips built a test rig with a bank of cambered slats for wings. It rose 50 feet. Encouraged, Phillips produced a version *(below)* with four banks of slats; it hopped some 500 feet in 1907, but by then aviation had passed Phillips by.

The umbrellaplane *(overleaf),* an American creation, had a circular, ribless wing mounted on spokes that radiated from a central engine. Several times in 1912 it flew around Cicero Field near Chicago, but it is best remembered as the first project of a young engineer who became a major aircraft designer, Chance Vought.

The 1908 multiplane at left, designed by the Marquis d'Equevilly, looked like a vegetable shredder—and flew like one.

The slender airfoils of Horatio Phillips' flying box resemble stacks of venetian blinds, but the craft flew briefly in 1907.

In the umbrellaplane, a circular wing surrounded the engine and pilot.

Movable drum wings protected this French pilot but failed to lift him.

Twelve years were devoted, in vain, to this German triplane of linen and bamboo.

Hopes for the 1908 Dorand, the first French plane designed for military use, ended when its towering wings could not lift it.

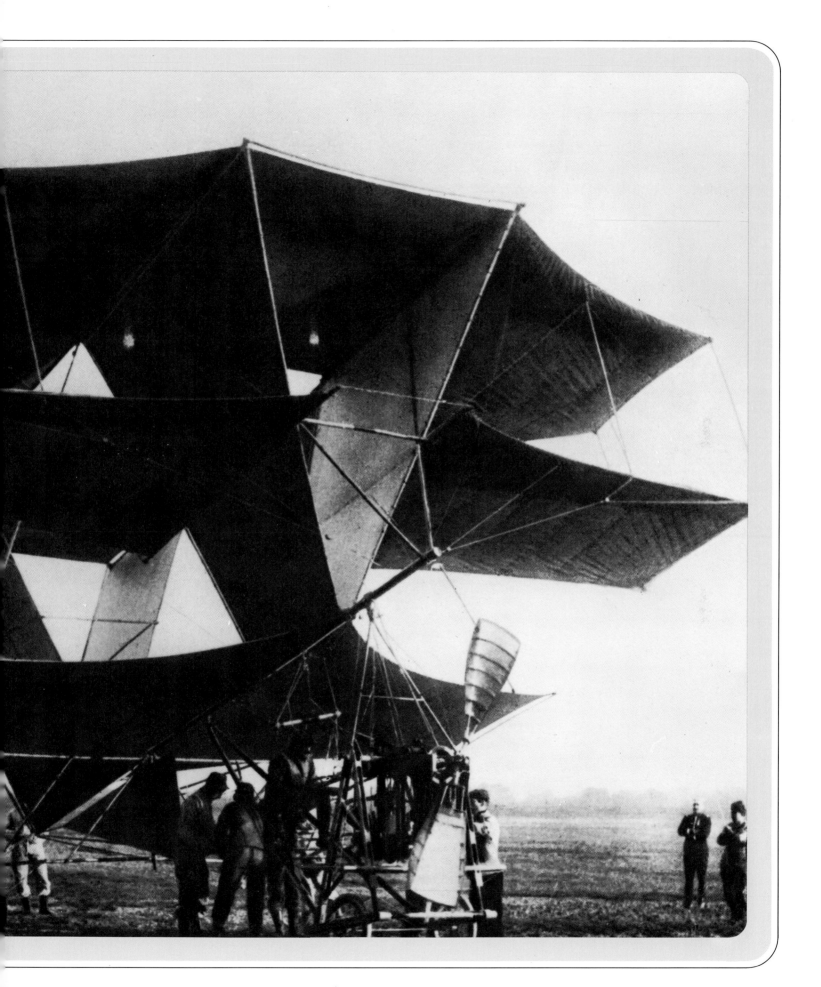

Professor Jerome S. Zerbe's craft, with five double-cambered wings, scoots across Dominguez Field (left) during the Los Angeles air meet of 1910. Underpowered to begin with, the taxiing plane hit a pothole and collapsed (below).

appointment of Albert F. Zahm as head of the Smithsonian's official observation team. Zahm was a reputable aeronautical engineer, but he had testified for Curtiss during the patent litigation.

The Buzzard, as the Langley relic was affectionately called around the Smithsonian, had deteriorated considerably since 1903. Many of its carefully hollowed-out ribs were beyond repair. Its five-cylinder radial engine—a particularly lovely piece of machinery about the diameter of a bicycle wheel and appearing almost as light—would deliver only three fourths of its rated 52 horsepower, despite the ministrations of its designer, Charles Manly, who came to Hammondsport to assist in the tests. (Manly had also been the pilot of the Langley machine in 1903.)

Six weeks of work put the Aerodrome in shape for a trial run. On the morning of May 28, 1914, Curtiss climbed into the pilot's seat suspended below the main wings. On pontoons that had been substituted for Langley's catapult launching gear, the plane taxied out into Keuka Lake. "Skimming over the wavelets, it headed into the wind, rose in level poise, soared gracefully for 150 feet, and landed softly on the water," Zahm, the official observer, wrote jubilantly. Five days later, the Buzzard made another short hop. That was sufficient for the Smithsonian, which subsequently claimed that the Langley Aerodrome, "without modification," had flown at last. "It has demonstrated that, with its original structure and power, it is capable of flying with a pilot and several hundred pounds of useful load. It is the first aeroplane in the history of the world of which this can truthfully be said."

Hardly. Curtiss had indeed flown the Aerodrome; photographs clearly showed it airborne. But it was not Langley's original machine. Curtiss and his crew, in secret, had made numerous alterations. A few of the more obvious changes, as Curtiss noted, actually detracted from the Aerodrome's ability to fly, "Three floats and their supports added 350 pounds of weight to the machine, not to mention the head resistance." But dozens of subtle modifications, many of them based on scientific data painstakingly accumulated by the Wright brothers, had been necessary to coax the Aerodrome into the sky.

The episode provoked Orville Wright to a fury. After comparing photographs of the old and new Aerodromes, he listed 35 changes, ranging from propeller shape to tail assembly but concentrating on the wing improvements, which were crucial:

"The wings of the Langley machine collapsed in 1903 not on account of a defect in the launching device, as Professor Langley thought, but because the trussing of the wings, due to the lack of knowledge at that time of the location of the center of pressure, was improperly placed. This trussing was moved 30 inches at Hammondsport to correct that error." Also, Orville noted, "the camber of the wings used in 1903 was 1 to 12; that used at Hammondsport in 1914 was 1 to 18. This change improves the dynamic efficiency of a wing over 30 per cent."

With the addition of a new 80-horsepower Curtiss engine, the Aerodrome underwent further tests at Hammondsport in 1915. As before, it could lift off the water, but turns aloft were another matter. Maneuverability trials were about to begin in June 1915 when a little, bespectacled man with a graying moustache and a camera drifted into the Curtiss camp. Hesitant to show himself around Hammondsport, he had registered at a hotel nine miles away under the name W. L. Oren. On the morning of June 5, as the Curtiss crew—Curtiss himself was not there—readied the Aerodrome for tests on Keuka Lake, the stranger watched from the shore, training his field glasses on the machine.

The machine gradually acquired speed, the intruder later reported, "ran about 800 feet and the rear wings broke near the middle on both sides and folded upwards. When I reached the hangars the machine had been towed to shore. I took four pictures of the machine when one of the workmen noticed me. About six or seven men gathered around and I was told they would not allow me to leave the grounds with the films. They did not want any pictures of the wreck taken 'on account of legal complications.' Seeing they were determined that I should not take the pictures away I surrendered the films. No one asked my name."

It was just as well—W. L. Oren had been Orville's older brother Lorin Wright, who had infiltrated the enemy camp to gather evidence that the Aerodrome had been changed.

As it turned out, the Hammondsport tests had no effect on the outcome of the Wrights' patent litigation. In October 1915, Orville, who had been buying up most of the Wright Company stock, sold out at a considerable profit. The new owners continued the lawsuit, but in July 1917, three months after the United States entered World War I, the government imposed a national pooling of aircraft patents. The result, as Grover Loening described it, was "to lay the Wright patent fight into a deep grave, never to rise again." Orville would continue to devote his life to aviation, serving as an honored adviser to a number of prestigious federal boards and private foundations for aeronautical research.

By 1920, Glenn Curtiss was on his way out of aviation, to become a Florida land developer. In 1929 the former Wright and Curtiss interests, both of which had gone through various ownerships, were merged as the Curtiss-Wright Corporation. The irony in the order of names was not lost on either man.

For Orville Wright, the battle was still not over. After Secretary Walcott's death in 1927 the Smithsonian Institution softened its claims for the Langley Aerodrome, but not enough to satisfy Orville. In 1925 he had sought an impartial investigation of the affair; by 1928, when it became apparent that none would be made, he sent the historic Kitty Hawk Flyer to Britain's Science Museum, in London. He explained that "in a foreign museum this machine will be a constant reminder of the reason for its being there."

Not until 1942 did the Smithsonian recant completely and express regret for both its conduct of the 1914 tests and the "misinformed" claims made for the Langley machine. Should the Wright Flyer be

The Langley Aerodrome flies from Keuka Lake in upstate New York after extensive modifications made in 1914. With its new Curtiss engine, changed wing design, added pontoons and a different cockpit position, the craft bore decreasing resemblance to the original version that crashed on launch in 1903.

returned to America for display, the Smithsonian promised, "it would be given the highest place of honor, which is its due."

With some persuasion from President Franklin D. Roosevelt, who in 1910 had watched the Wright exhibition team fly at Boston, Orville attended a dinner in Washington on December 17, 1943—the 40th anniversary of Kitty Hawk—at which his agreement to the return of the plane was announced. The announcement was not made by Orville. Characteristically, he was silent through most of the evening.

Five years later the Wright Flyer came home at last and was given its promised display in the Smithsonian. The dedication plaque pays unqualified tribute to the two brothers who "by original scientific research . . . discovered the principles of human flight" and who "as inventors, builders and fliers . . . taught man to fly, and opened the era of aviation."

Orville was not present for the December 17, 1948, dedication ceremony; 11 months earlier he had died of a heart attack, at the age of 76. Curtiss had died in 1930, at the age of 52. Years before, he had written to a friend: "The honors bestowed upon the Wrights and the credit which is due them is not because of their patent, but because of their achievement." It was a just tribute, from a man they hated. ❧

A fan made in Paris for a New York restaurateur shows a fashionable aviatrix about to take off from a busy airfield.

The enameled cover of a pencil box made in Germany contrasts horsepower with the romance of powered flight.

This combination clock and barometer commemorates the 1909 crossing of the English Channel with a brass model of Blériot in his monoplane.

A Wright biplane skims above sailing vessels in a scene enameled on this French silver cigarette case of about 1910.

Marketing the air fad

As the second decade of the 20th Century began, the romance of aviation had captured the imagination of much of the world. People were moved by the saga of gallant aviators challenging the elements in their uncertain machines. Though few could actually expect to fly, almost anyone, with the eager help of craftsmen, artists and businessmen, could enjoy aviation vicariously. Pictures of flight began to appear on ladies' fans and gentlemen's cigarette cases, on fine porcelain and, inevitably, on merchants' promotional giveaways.

Children were among the first to catch the dream; they began to play with model airplanes (some of which were exhibited at the great aviation exposition in Paris in 1909), with aviator dolls and with aviation games, toys and puzzles of all kinds. Their enthusiasm was infectious, and when a family gathered around the piano of an evening, it might be heard to sing "Come Josephine in My Flying Machine" or perhaps "Take Me Down to Squantum, I Want to See Them Fly" *(page 140)*.

This Royal Doulton jug, part of a set made in England about 1911, shows planes rounding a pylon during a great air meet.

A monoplane joins birds in flight on this Royal Nippon ginger jar, part of a set produced about 1910 in England.

Aeronautical china given away as a promotion by a Pennsylvania merchant included this calendar bowl.

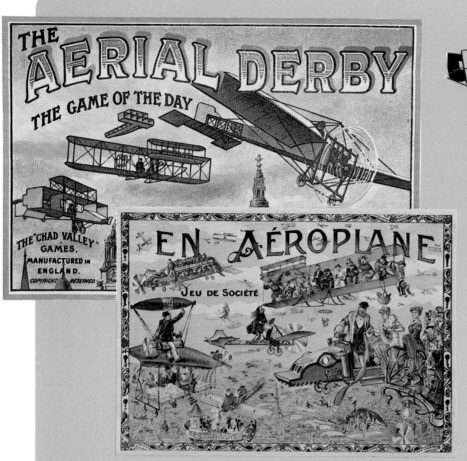

Board games with aerial themes, played by rolling dice and moving pieces, intrigued youngsters in England and France.

In this French game two biplanes circle while a ball dropped through the roof of the "airplane factory" knocks over pins.

A German toy, modeled on the Blériot monoplane, had a paper propeller that spun and improbable tin wings that flapped.

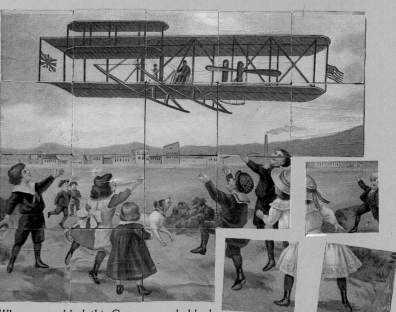

A windup roundabout made in Germany
for the American market spins tin biplanes
and dirigibles around a central pylon.

Two German bisque figures, shown here
in their actual size, display the clothing that
well-dressed aviators wore in 1910.

When assembled, this German-made block
puzzle shows children greeting a biplane that
flies British and American flags.

Songwriters responded eagerly to the growing popularity of aviation, as this sheet music from six nations demonstrates. The tunes saluted flying heroes, real and imaginary. Some gave a new twist to old themes, as in the German "Flying Love" (this page, left center); others celebrated the joy of flying, as in the Russian song "In an Airplane" (far left, center) and "Airplane Flight through the Merry World" (this page, bottom), published in Prague.

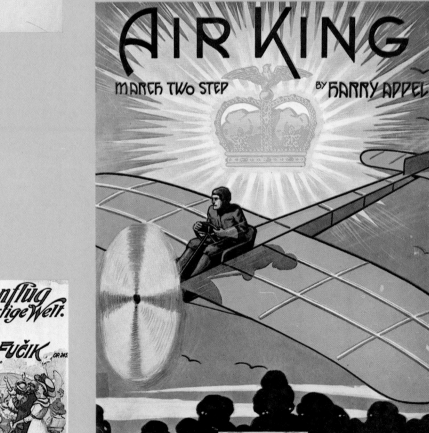

N° 4. Juillet 1913

Prix : Un Franc

LA SCIENCE ET LA VIE

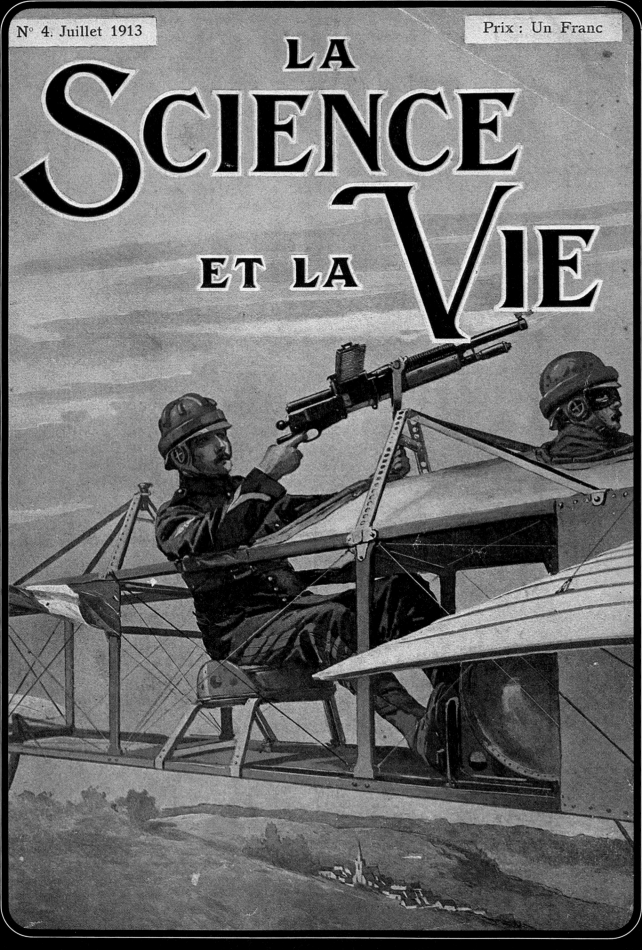

5

Marshaling aviation for war

On the morning of September 21, 1913, several hundred journalists and invited spectators gathered at a flying field near Buc, France, to watch a performance by Adolphe Pégoud, an aviator whom the press—with some justification—had dubbed "the foolhardy one." The onlookers had been drawn to the dusty airdrome by the promise of "something new" from Pégoud, and they had ample reason to believe that he would not disappoint them.

In a flight three weeks earlier, at Juvisy, the unassuming little man with a shy smile and a handlebar mustache had deliberately flipped his plane on its back—in those days, usually a prelude to a crash. But instead of plunging to earth, Pégoud had flown for more than 500 yards upside down, as if it were an ordinary maneuver, and then righted his plane. Next day he repeated the trick to show that it had been no fluke.

The demonstration had astonished the aviation world but left Pégoud unfulfilled. He announced that he was not satisfied with merely flying upside down. And now at Buc, as the press waited expectantly, he was ready with another stunt.

Pégoud began with a warm-up flight that one reporter described as "a wild dance in the air." He surrendered himself, the reporter wrote, "to all those fantasies that the most fertile imagination is capable of inventing. One saw him slide on the tail, then on the wing, fall headfirst, fly completely inclined on one side, then upside down. Each of these daring feats ended with a perfect recovery, and not once did the amazed spectators have the impression that the aviator was in the least danger, so fully did the man seem master of himself and his machine."

Then Pégoud climaxed his performance with a maneuver previously considered to be more than either an airplane's structure or a pilot's composure could bear. From a height of 10,500 feet, he pushed his Blériot XI over into a screaming, head-first dive to gather speed; then, as the journalist saw it, "making a magnificent curve and continuing his flight, carried by the acquired speed, he climbed straight up toward the sky, hovered an instant upside down and let himself fall again to finally recover his horizontal position."

Pégoud had done an inside loop, describing a vertical circle of some 400 yards in diameter. With that feat he established himself as the premier aerial performer of his day, the world's first true acrobatic pilot.

It has since been acknowledged that Pégoud was not the very first man to loop an airplane; a month earlier, an obscure Russian military

The military theme of a 1913 French magazine, Science and Life, was symptomatic of a new role developing for aviation as part of the arms race that was thrusting Europe toward war.

pilot named Peter Nesterov, out for a joy ride, had impulsively done the same stunt—and had been promptly put under house arrest for endangering government property. But Pégoud, for all his showmanship, was much more than a one-shot daredevil out to please a crowd. Behind his stunts lay a serious purpose—to probe the frontiers of performance by man and machine. He deliberately threw himself into situations previously considered suicidal—and then demonstrated to his own satisfaction, and for the benefit of other pilots, that he could pull himself out.

"It seemed important to me to prove to my comrades that they should never believe themselves lost," Pégoud wrote. "I would like to say: 'My friends, you have seen me fly upside down; you know that it is possible. Consequently, if the day comes when, in a dive, your plane goes over on its back, let it do it. Deliberately, calmly, take your time and straighten it up, using the controls as if you were flying normally.' "

The inspiration for Pégoud's aerial acrobatics had come earlier in 1913 during his tenure as a test pilot for the irrepressible Louis Blériot. Pégoud had applied for the job after serving a hitch in the French Army. He had been flying only a few months, but Blériot overlooked his inexperience when it became apparent that the young pilot possessed, in aviators' jargon, "hands"—an innate feel for flying.

Pégoud's first job for Blériot was to test a new hook-and-cable system for landing planes on a ship at sea. He next attempted to become the first pilot to parachute out of his plane. The scheme called for him to pop his chute before getting out of the cockpit. On the first tug the parachute opened as planned, dragging Pégoud the length of the fuselage and giving him "a good whack of the stabilizer on the shoulder," as he put it, before he fell clear.

Bruised but intact, Pégoud floated down into a tree. The abandoned airplane, however, kept on flying. Pégoud watched it from his perch. "My old crate," he recalled, "did tricks on its own." Those unguided tricks—a dive, a vertical climb, a wing-slip, then another dive, with the plane righting itself between gyrations before plunging finally to the ground—convinced Pégoud that a strong, well-balanced machine, in the hands of a cool-headed pilot, could execute maneuvers formerly considered impossible.

He set out methodically to prove his thesis. First he trained on the ground for the moves he anticipated making in the air: Strapped into the cockpit of a plane that was inverted on sawhorses, Pégoud hung head down for 20 minutes at a time, gradually getting accustomed to the confusing physical sensations of being upside down. To a standard Blériot monoplane he added extra wing bracing and a larger tail area that promised better response. Then he took to the air, slowly and carefully developing the intricate maneuvers that would make up his repertoire. Brimming with confidence after preliminary trials, Pégoud in September put on the bravura performance at Buc, climaxed by the loop. Word of it quickly spread around the world.

More than a few of Pégoud's fellow aviators were skeptical when they

Three maneuvers pioneered by French pilot Adolphe Pégoud—looping the loop, a sideways rollover and a backward dive —are diagramed in a 1913 magazine. The diagram mistakenly shows the plane performing an outside loop, which was not accomplished until 1927; the drawing should show the pilot's head on the inside of the loop, the wheels outside.

heard the news of his latest stunt. He convinced them by going on the road as a one-man show, performing in a short space of time in Britain, Germany, Belgium, Austria, Italy, Rumania, the Netherlands and Russia. Pilots around the world began to imitate him. Lincoln Beachey, the leading stunt pilot in the United States, was incensed that he had not been the first to do a loop. Beachey, who had learned to fly from Glenn Curtiss in 1911, had become wildly popular for a chilling collection of stunts that included a vertical dive with no hands on the control wheel. He had also been the first man in the United States to fly upside down without crashing. Hearing of Pégoud's feat, Beachey immediately ordered a specially built Curtiss biplane in order to put loops into his own repertoire.

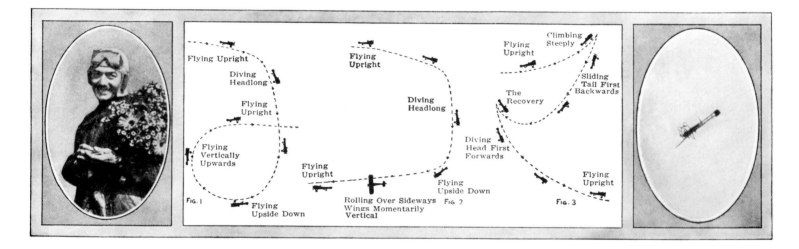

Within six months, Beachey and some 50 other aviators, including 28 Frenchmen and 11 Englishmen, had looped successfully. But nobody relished aerial acrobatics more than Pégoud. In a memorable paean to flying, he wrote: "To play with the elements of the air in any position and for any length of time, to let my machine go like a cork bobbing on a rough sea, to handle all the treacheries of the atmosphere, to tame them and put myself back on the ground gracefully, with calm and confidence, that is my supreme happiness."

As Pégoud had hoped, his exploits generated a new confidence among his fellow aviators. The little Frenchman had dared the unknown and demonstrated that it was not so frightening after all. He had shown that the treacheries of the atmosphere, as he called them, could be mastered. Not since Wilbur Wright demonstrated his Flyer at Le Mans in 1908 had one man so affected the flying art. From the acrobatics that Pégoud pioneered would grow the aerial maneuvers that all too soon became the standard evasion tactics for combat pilots in World War I.

Pégoud's own career was brutally cut short by that war. He was only 26 and had been flying less than three years in all when, on August 31, 1915, he was shot down in combat with a German plane over Alsace. In time, Pégoud's flying comrades acknowledged their debt to him and he became recognized as the patron saint of the fighter pilot.

In contrast to the heroism and tragedy of World War I's aerial encounters, the first appearances of the airplane over a battlefield were almost larks. The distinction of being the first fliers to observe war from the air may belong to the studious Roland Garros, the raffish Charlie Hamilton and their fellow members of the Moisant International Aviators, an exhibition troupe founded by John and Alfred Moisant. In February 1911, the troupe was performing in Mexico during a revolution, and the pilots decided to have a look at the hostilities. The troupe's manager arranged an air show for the government's Army, and Garros, Hamilton and the others playfully pitched oranges at the soldiers, who responded to the mock bombing by firing blanks at the planes.

Hamilton, however, itched for more serious action. "Flying over the troops at the battle of Juarez," he boasted later, "I could have destroyed all the forces, federal and insurgent, in a single day, had I been provided with bombs."

Later that year, airplanes did go into combat with the Italian Army, which was waging a colonial war with Turkey in North Africa. In October, Captain Carlo Piazza, who had won the 1911 Circuit of Italy, flew a scouting mission over the Turkish lines in Libya (then part of the Otto-

A postcard commemorates the squadron of 12 Italian aviators, commanded by Captain Carlo Montù (far left), who flew the world's first combat missions over Libya in 1911. Their assignments included reconnaissance and bombing.

LA FLOTTIGLIA
degli AVIATORI VOLONTARI
in CIRENAICA

man Empire). A week later, Lieutenant Giulio Gavotti led a contingent of Italian planes on history's first live bombing run. Gavotti's four bombs were grenades that he carried in a leather bag. When he reached his target areas, a Turkish encampment and a vital oasis, he fitted detonators into the grenades as he held his Taube monoplane on course with his knees, then tossed the missiles out. By all evidence, the raid caused more consternation than carnage.

The seriocomic aspect of early aerial warfare vanished soon enough. During the Balkan War of 1913, Greek pilots came under harassing fire from Turkish ground troops. That same year, after two Spanish pilots were seriously wounded by Moroccan riflemen over Tetuan, near Tangier, the British magazine *Flight* sounded a warning: "It has been said that aircraft form almost impossible targets either for artillery or riflemen, but it would look as though in this case the hostile Moors had either a great deal of luck with their shooting, or that an aeroplane on the wing is not so hard to hit as we had imagined."

Since 1911, the European powers had been building up their air arms for the larger conflict that, with increasing certainty, lay ahead. By the beginning of 1912, the French Army, the most air-minded in Europe, had increased its fleet of planes to 254. In June of that year French aircraft manufacturers staged a two-day competition that was designed to demonstrate the value of their airplanes to the military. The Circuit of Anjou, as the contest was called, covered 97 miles between the towns of Angers, Saumur and Cholet in the province of Anjou, a triangular course that was to be completed seven times. Such a marathon was intended to test the mettle of planes and pilots by simulating the grueling conditions of wartime.

A welter of military attachés from various European nations converged on Angers, the starting point. Civilian spectators from all over the Continent swarmed through the streets, and for a few days little Angers was a boom town, its cafés filled to overflowing, hotels jammed and landlords inflating their prices mercilessly.

Also gathered at Angers were France's best pilots and its most advanced flying machines. Outstanding even in this company, and the popular favorite to collect the 50,000-franc grand prize, was the sleek, powerful Deperdussin designed by Louis Béchereau, who later would engineer the famous Spad fighter of World War I. The Deperdussin was the first plane to be built with a monocoque fuselage, a shell-like construction that required no internal bracing. The plane's namesake and owner, Armand Deperdussin, was a wealthy industrialist. Within a year Deperdussin would be in deep financial trouble that would lead to his conviction for fraud, but for now he had grandly taken over a floor of Angers's best hotel for his sales representatives and public relations personnel. Outside town, his planes were on public display in a cavernous hangar.

The most likely challenger to the Deperdussin was the Nieuport, a creation of the French engineer Édouard Nieuport. Although derived

The advance guard of air combat

Developed in peacetime, these highly original planes pioneered the roles of fighter, bomber and scout, siring the military aircraft that would come of age in World War I. They are shown in scale (approximately six feet to one inch).

The Wright Military Flyer was the first plane bought by the United States Army; an improved version was the first to have weapons test-fired from it (its stability was not affected). The United States Navy's first plane, the Curtiss A-1, was also the first practical seaplane.

England's fast-climbing B.S.1, a constantly evolving test plane, was the prototype of the single-seated fighter. The father of the heavy bomber was Sikorsky's *Russky Vityaz*, the first operational four-engined plane. But the first bombs were dropped in war from the Taube, a plane so stable the pilot could let go the controls to drop grenades.

MILITARY FLYER—WRIGHT BROTHERS (1909)
Known as Signal Corps No. 1, the Military Flyer had two seats next to a 30-hp engine on the lower wing, enabling the pilot to carry an observer or gunner.

CURTISS A-1—GLENN CURTISS (1911)
Modified from Curtiss' 1909 Rheims Flyer, the A-1 had a main center float and smaller floats under each wing. With retractable wheels, it became an amphibian.

B.S.1—GEOFFREY DE HAVILLAND (1913)

Powered by a 100-hp Gnôme engine and streamlined with a monocoque fuselage, the B.S.1 (for Blériot Scout) could achieve a top speed of 92 mph.

TAUBE—IGO ETRICH (1910)

Designed with a novel wing-warping system, the birdlike Taube (German for dove) was eventually built by 10 firms in Germany and Austria. This 1914 model had a water-cooled Daimler-Mercedes engine.

RUSSKY VITYAZ—IGOR SIKORSKY (1913)

After experimenting with four Argus engines in tandem push-pull sets, Sikorsky mounted them next to one another on the leading edge of the bottom wing, thus launching the era of the big bomber.

from the Blériot, the Nieuport had a flatter wing camber for greater speed, and a smooth, rounded cowling that reduced drag.

But success in the Circuit of Anjou would not hinge on design innovations. An unforeseen element, the weather, would turn the race into a contest far different from any that had been envisioned.

June 16, the first day of the race, dawned calm, but soon the wind rose, bringing a full-fledged storm. Wind whistled through the bracing wires of the airplanes tethered at the flying field outside Angers, and black clouds spat a stinging rain. Inside a hangar, the pilots wrangled over whether the race should be run. The brawling Parisian Jules Védrines, who was flying for Deperdussin, climbed onto a fuel can and shouted for a boycott. Most of the other pilots backed him, but one, Roland Garros, had no intention of withdrawing.

At 8:45 a.m., Garros had his plane pushed to the starting line. The Blériot shook from the most violent gusts yet and a member of Garros' entourage tried to dissuade him: "Don't you think it better to wait a little?" he suggested. Another friend answered for Garros: "Don't think about it. He knows he must go."

Those words, Garros said later, "filled my veins with the enthusiasm I needed. It seemed to me that I was going for a small walk in the rain." A mechanic turned the propeller, the Gnôme engine coughed to life and Garros took off toward Cholet.

Garros battled the wind around the course. From his seat in the bucking Blériot he could look down at trees bent double under the force of the gale. The rain pelted his face like needles and clouded his goggles. His hands, wrists and arms grew dangerously stiff from fighting the controls. Garros had gambled on the weather improving; instead, it grew worse on the second circuit and he found himself flying blindly through a continuous, drenching storm. "I controlled the plane with one hand and shielded myself with the other," he said. "I could see absolutely nothing and navigated solely by compass. Finally I saw a hole in the clouds, landed in a small field and asked a farmer where I was. He gave me directions and I took off again."

Blocking his path in the distance, however, was an ominously dark wall of clouds. "I advanced," Garros continued, "flew closer and closer to the black barrier and then reached its center—a torrent of hail. My goal, the aerodrome at Angers, was underneath the storm. Eyes half closed, furiously maneuvering my controls, I wove between the roofs and chimneys of the town. This was my last effort. Suddenly the silhouette of hangars and grandstands came into view, and I cut the ignition and landed."

Garros was astonished to learn from his crew that only one other Circuit of Anjou contestant was still in the running. Only six of the 34 other entrants had dared follow him into the storm, and five of them had dropped out, victims of airsickness, engine trouble and crash landings. By the time Garros went up again on his third and final circuit of the day, the skies had cleared and the wind had died; he completed the

A 1903 poster reminiscent of his Wild West days features Samuel Cody—not related to Buffalo Bill Cody—and one of the giant kites he flew before building England's first successful airplane.

course without incident. The next day, in sunny skies, he made four more circuits and claimed the grand prize.

Two months after the Circuit of Anjou, Great Britain held its first military-aircraft trials at Larkhill, on Salisbury Plain. The British had been slow getting into military aviation, but at the urging of such hawkish politicians as Winston Churchill the government was now making up for lost time. In April of 1912 the Royal Flying Corps was established, to serve both the Army and the Navy, and by offering £8,600 in prizes at the military trials in August, Britain clearly was hoping to tap into the best available aviation technology, both domestic and foreign.

Appropriately, the winning pilot at Larkhill was the naturalized Briton Samuel Cody, whose British Army Aeroplane No. 1 had been the first heavier-than-air machine to fly in Britain, in October 1908. Papa Cody, as the English press fondly called him, was the oldest of the earliest aviators—he was 47 when he first flew an airplane. Before that he had been a cowboy in his native Texas, a gold prospector in the Klondike and a Wild West showman on the English theatrical circuit. Cody never lost his cowboy manner: He had shoulder-length hair, wore Western boots and a 10-gallon hat, and carried a Colt revolver that he sometimes used to shoot open locked hangar doors; once he righted an upended airplane by lassoing its tail skid.

Cody could neither read nor write. But he had an instinctive flair for

Samuel Cody's Army Aeroplane No. 1, being hauled out for flight in 1908, was the largest yet built, with a 52-foot wingspan. It was nicknamed the Flying Cathedral.

aeronautical engineering. Earlier he had built and flown huge kites capable of lifting a man, and their military potential for artillery spotting had so intrigued the War Office that Cody was hired as kiting instructor at the Army Balloon Factory. There he also helped to build Britain's first Army dirigible, the *Nulli Secundus (Second to None),* which made one triumphal flight over London in 1907 before being caught in the open by a gale, deflated and carted home. The *Nulli Secundus* never flew again, but its Antoinette engine became the power plant for the airplane Cody was building on his own.

Army Aeroplane No. 1 and Cody's subsequent machines were huge biplanes popularly known as Flying Cathedrals—both for their size and for their drooping, cathedral-angled lower wings. Relatively clumsy and difficult to fly, the planes contributed little to aircraft design, but Cody himself, like Ferber in France, had been an enormous stimulus to the progress of British aviation. By the time of Cody's triumph in 1912, the balloon factory at Farnborough had been transformed into the Royal

Workers man their stations at the Albatros Works, the first German aircraft factory to use mass-production techniques. Albatros' output, which was tied to the growth of Germany's armed forces, increased from 12 planes in 1911 to 338 in 1914.

Aircraft Factory and was attracting a number of talented designers.

In that same year a privately owned British company introduced the world's first fully enclosed cabin biplanes and monoplanes. They were the work of Alliott Verdon Roe, a onetime merchant-marine engineer who had first studied flight by watching sea birds on the wing and then building model gliders to imitate them. In 1913, Roe went on to produce the Avro 504, a stagger-winged biplane that became enormously popular as a military trainer. Turned out by the thousands, the 504 was one of the most widely sold—and longest-lived—machines ever built; later models were still flying in the early 1930s.

The work of two other men who would have a lasting impact on British aircraft design, Geoffrey de Havilland and T. O. M. Sopwith, also began to emerge at this time. Sopwith, an aristocratic young yachtsman, had flown in European and American air meets before turning to the drawing board. De Havilland, the son of a clergyman, had taken up aviation after a stint as a designer of double-decker London city buses. As a member of the government design team at Farnborough, de Havilland was chiefly responsible for the B.S.1, a trim and speedy (92-mile-per-hour) little biplane that appeared in 1912. It was the forerunner of the classic single-seated scout and fighter biplanes to come. Deriving from the B.S.1 came Sopwith's 1913 Tabloid scout; highly maneuverable and able to climb to 15,000 feet in 10 minutes, the Tabloid established the well-designed biplane as superior to any monoplane of the day. The Tabloid, in turn, evolved into the 115-mile-per-hour Sopwith Camel, one of the most effective fighters of World War I.

Like the British, the Germans had lagged years behind the French in perceiving the wartime potential of the airplane. The first heavier-than-air flight in Germany was made in 1908 by a visiting Dane, J. C. H. Ellehammer, and received scant notice. Germans were so intrigued with the rigid dirigibles developed by Count Ferdinand von Zeppelin that, for a time, little private or government money went into airplane development. Then, in an effort to catch up, the fledgling German aircraft industry began borrowing freely from French designs: the German Aviatik biplane was modeled on the French Farman, the Euler on the Voisin, and the Albatros on both the Farman and another French plane, the Sommer. In the same vein, Germany bought manufacturing rights to the distinctive bird-winged Taube (Dove) monoplane, which had been designed by an Austrian, Igo Etrich, and was used by the Italians against the Turks in Libya.

The Germans also acquired one of aviation's improvisational geniuses in the person of a brash and very young Dutchman named Anthony Fokker. The son of a wealthy coffee planter from the East Indies, Tony Fokker had gone to Germany to study engineering; in 1910, at the age of 20, he and an associate borrowed from known technology to build a wing-warping monoplane that managed a 100-foot hop. In two years' time, Fokker had started his own flying school and, as a would-be

The Wunderkind of German aviation, Dutch-born Anthony Fokker, built and flew his first plane in 1910 when he was 20 years old. "It was pure elation," he exulted after the flight. "I felt like Balboa when he sighted the Pacific."

airplane manufacturer, was hustling for German Army contracts.

Fokker was a natural showman and a brilliant demonstration pilot; as an aircraft designer he took ideas where he found them. When a lightweight French-built Morane-Saulnier monoplane landed at Berlin's Johannisthal airfield in 1913, Fokker closely observed its design and later bought a junked model of the same plane for further study. Substituting welded steel-tube construction for wood in the fuselage, improving the Morane-Saulnier's wing structure and splaying the wheels outward—to correct its tendency to make the dangerous, uncontrolled turn on takeoff or landing called a ground loop—he produced the Fokker M.5. It was the progenitor of the famous Fokker single-seated monoplane fighter series that two years later would dominate the skies over the Western Front.

On the eastern edge of Europe, Igor Sikorsky, a graduate of the Russian naval academy at St. Petersburg, had begun experimenting in 1908 with a helicopter. Discouraged when his 25-horsepower Anzani engine failed to deliver enough lifting power to the rotor blades, Sikorsky turned to designing a series of large fixed-winged machines—the world's first practical four-engined planes. In 1913, Sikorsky's efforts bore remarkable fruit: the Ilya Mourometz, a magnificent four-engined biplane with a wingspan of 113 feet, an enclosed passenger cabin equipped with pantry, toilet and interior heating, and even an outside promenade deck. After seeing the Ilya Mourometz at a 1914 military review, Czar Nicholas II ordered 10 of the imperial-looking giants for the Russian Air Service, including some with floats for use by the Russian Navy; after the War began, 70 more were added to the Czar's air fleet.

In contrast to the European powers, the United States devoted minuscule amounts of money and attention to military aviation in the prewar years. Isolated by the broad Atlantic from the political tremors that were shaking the Continent, Americans felt no urgent need to build an air force; as late as 1913, the United States government was spending less than Bulgaria on military aviation. Some funds were available for experimentation, however, and the military services made good use of them. In 1911, the United States Army conducted the world's first live-bomb tests from a standard Wright biplane. During the same year, an American Army lieutenant, Riley Scott, produced the world's first bombsight. And it was the United States Navy—with an assist from Glenn Curtiss—that launched naval aviation in the winter of 1910-1911 with the first successful shipboard takeoffs and landings.

On November 14, 1910, in Hampton Roads, Virginia, Curtiss exhibition pilot Eugene Ely clattered down a sloping 83-foot wooden platform atop the forward deck of the cruiser U.S.S. *Birmingham*. Dropping precariously from the ship's bow to the wave tops, so close that he splashed his rudder and propeller tips and drenched himself thoroughly, Ely flew through thick fog to a safe landing on the shore two and a

Igor Sikorsky's big Ilya Mourometz, named for a Russian hero, lands in 1914 with two passengers at attention on the exposed observation deck.

National subscription campaigns used patriotic art, such as the German postcard at left, the appeal "Give wings to Italy," above, and the poster for a French concert at right, to solicit the donations that supported Europe's first military air services.

half miles away. Two months later, on January 18, 1911, he made the first trip in the other direction, flying out from the Presidio grounds overlooking San Francisco Bay to alight on a 30-by-125-foot platform on the quarterdeck of the cruiser U.S.S. *Pennsylvania*. After lunch on board with the skipper, Ely flew back to San Francisco.

His pioneering flights, however modest, presaged an era in which great aircraft carriers would roam the world's oceans, launching combat planes at targets on land and sea. But few people at the time envisioned the modern carrier. Glenn Curtiss, in fact, believed that the future of naval aviation belonged to airplanes that could take off and land on water and be lifted on board ship for storage by means of a hoist. Most senior Navy officers agreed, and Curtiss, with his customary eye for business, set out to oblige them.

Eight days after Ely's landing on the *Pennsylvania* in 1911, Curtiss unveiled the world's first practical seaplane. In the design of its floats, Curtiss' plane owed a debt to a canard-type hydroplane that had been tested the previous year in a Mediterranean harbor near Marseilles by a French inventor, Henri Fabre. With its skeletal body attached to tandem wings above and floats underneath, Fabre's plane looked like a section of flying fence. Underpowered, it never flew more than four miles.

But Curtiss' sturdy machine, a biplane with a single pontoon substituting for the wheeled landing gear, "seemed to leap into the air like a frightened gull," as Curtiss jubilantly reported after his first flight. Almost immediately, he followed the seaplane with an amphibian, the Triad, whose retractable, hand-cranked wheels and flotation gear offered a choice of land- or water-based operation. Curtiss' innovative craft aroused the interest of navies everywhere; by 1913, Curtiss seaplanes and amphibians were flying with the Russian, German and Japanese fleets as well as with the American.

Curtiss went on to produce yet another variety of waterborne air-

plane, a flying boat, whose watertight fuselage resembled the hull of a motorboat. Like his pontoon planes, Curtiss' flying boat was immediately successful and widely copied. Affluent sportsmen, in particular, were fascinated by the "aerial yacht." The heir to the International Harvester farm equipment fortune, Harold McCormick, was among the first to buy one, a two-seater; he used it to commute between his estate in Lake Forest, Illinois, and his office in Chicago. By the end of 1913, Curtiss had sold more than 40 flying boats, and other aircraft manufacturers had hastened to introduce their own lines of watercraft.

Though it galled Orville, the Wright Company too felt compelled to follow Curtiss' lead into seaplanes. By mid-1912 the company was bidding for a share of the market with a float-equipped Model C biplane. Later, Wright engineer Grover Loening designed a short-hulled flying boat under Orville's supervision. "He would never have approved of the flying boat," Loening said, "if its appearance had not been so totally different from the Curtiss boat that was sweeping the field."

The development of the seaplane attested to the accelerating progress being made in aviation in the years just before World War I. Month by month, the airplane grew more sophisticated, gaining in power, size and reliability—attributes that enabled adventurous pilots to attempt voyages of astonishing distance. In 1913 a 20-year-old Frenchman, Marcel Brindejonc des Moulinais, flew a Morane-Saulnier monoplane some 870 miles from France to Poland in a single day. He ate breakfast in Paris, lunch in Berlin and dinner in Warsaw—a pace that foreshadowed modern international air travel. Also in 1913, Jules Védrines flew 2,500 miles with a passenger from Nancy, in eastern France, to Cairo, with stops en route.

The reliability of engine and airframe underwent another test in 1913 when Roland Garros, the hero of Anjou, attempted an unprecedented nonstop flight across the Mediterranean Sea. Garros planned to fly southward from the French Riviera, vaulting the islands of Corsica and Sardinia, to land on the North African coast—a journey of some 512 miles, mostly over open water.

Garros knew the risks involved. His Morane-Saulnier land plane could carry only enough fuel for an eight-hour flight. If he was favored by a tail wind, which was anything but a sure bet, he calculated that the trip would take six and a half hours. When he reached Cagliari on the southernmost tip of Sardinia, he would have to make a crucial decision: to fly on over open sea to Africa, trusting that his fuel would hold out, or to land and refuel—and thus admit defeat.

Garros refused the offer of a French naval escort; such assistance, he decided, would crimp his freedom to choose his own departure time. (Nevertheless, French torpedo boats stationed themselves at points along his route.)

On September 23, 1913, near the seaside town of St. Raphael, Garros snugged an inner tube around his waist, fastened a red cloth to a fishing rod for use as a distress flag and at 5:47 a.m. took off, headed for Tunis. An hour and a half out, flying at 5,000 feet, Garros was numb with cold and growing drowsy when the noise of breaking metal jolted him awake. "Suddenly the whole machine started shaking and a hole appeared at the top of the engine cowling," he recalled. "Drops of oil seeped through and were thrown into my face by the wind. Obviously one of the motor parts had come off. Why didn't it stop?"

The Gnôme rotary engine kept turning, and Garros, resisting the temptation to put down in Corsica, which was visible to his left, flew on toward Sardinia and the point of no return, trying by "feverish" mental mathematics to calculate whether he would have fuel enough to reach the North African shore. As the fuel gauge dropped, he tried to estimate his air speed, with little success. "Was I moving forward or was I in a strong head wind that was slowing me down or blowing me off course? I hadn't the slightest idea." He tried to cheer himself up: "A head wind? Why not a tail wind? You never think of that!"

Gradually Garros became accustomed to the engine vibrations that continued to rack his plane. Over Sardinia he ran into head winds that slowed his speed and thick clouds that forced him to fly close to the sea. Finally he spotted Cagliari, the last possible landing place before the stretch of open sea, beyond which lay Africa.

"An agonizing dilemma: Would I land or go on?" Garros thought to himself: "I was almost an hour behind schedule; my fuel reserves were exhausted, and above all, I had a motor that had been running for five hours minus one of its parts.

"I hadn't yet made up my mind," Garros continued. "To land was to tarnish this crossing, to spoil a dream. I'll never forget that moment of hesitation. Then a strange force, stronger than my reason or my will, pulled me out to sea."

Garros made it to Africa, though not quite to his destination at Tunis. With his engine still knocking, he came down at Bizerte, 37 miles up the coast, at 1:40 p.m. It had been a close shave—he had flown for almost eight hours, six and a half of them with an engine that, on inspection, turned out to have lost a valve spring. On landing he had just five liters of fuel left in the tank, enough for another 10 or 12 minutes, but no more.

The epic flights of 1913 erased imaginary barriers to aerial achievement and opened the possibility of still-bolder journeys. Even a transoceanic flight was no longer inconceivable, and Lord Northcliffe of the London *Daily Mail* came up with a proposal that stirred the imagination: He offered £10,000 for the first airplane flight across the Atlantic.

Northcliffe's challenge was immediately controversial. No engine of the day was considered reliable enough for such a test, and no airplane could carry enough fuel to cross the Atlantic, even on the shortest route—1,900 miles from Newfoundland to Ireland. The contest rules required the crossing to be completed in 72 hours or less with no touchdowns for fueling en route except on water. This virtually ex-

Roland Garros is featured as a champion on a 1911 magazine cover despite repeated second-place finishes. Two years later he lived up to the billing by becoming the first to fly nonstop across the Mediterranean.

cluded land planes, and the most experienced aviators—Roland Garros among them—doubted that any existing seaplane could make it either. A seaplane's heavy floats added weight that might better be used to carry fuel, and there was the danger that the floats themselves might break up during any attempted landing on the seldom-placid Atlantic. But the problem that loomed largest, as Garros pointed out, was that of navigation. On his Mediterranean flight, islands had served as guideposts to help keep him on course. "After 800 kilometers," he noted wryly, "the African coast was unmissable." There were no such landmarks in the Atlantic—only vast stretches of featureless ocean. A small storm or a steady crosswind might throw a plane fatally off course.

Despite such perils, a host of contenders announced their intention of attempting an Atlantic crossing. Among them were France's premier

A showman primed for business

In 1908, Glenn Luther Martin, a successful 22-year-old automobile dealer, began working nights in an abandoned church in Santa Ana, California, often by the light of an oil lamp held patiently by his mother. A year later he rolled out his handmade creation, a Curtiss-type pusher biplane, and coaxed it a few feet into the air.

"Call him off before he is killed," pleaded a friend of the family, but Martin had found his element. Soon he was sporting fancy black leather flying clothes, taking film stars up for joy rides and hunting coyotes and escaped convicts from the air.

But the knack for showmanship that made Martin one of America's most publicized fliers was matched by his skill as a designer and businessman. When in 1914 the United States Army grounded all its Wright and Curtiss pusher biplanes following a rash of fatal accidents, Martin was ready with a plane, and a factory in Los Angeles, to fill the gap. The Army made his Model TT dual-controlled tractor biplane its standard trainer.

Dubbed the "Flying Dude" for his stylish attire, Glenn Martin grins over the carcass of a coyote he had chased down in his biplane.

stunt pilot Adolphe Pégoud; Enea Bossi, Italy's pioneer seaplane designer; and the noted German Albatros pilot Hellmuth Hirth, winner of a 325-mile race from Berlin to Vienna in 1912. In England, an enterprising young designer named Frederick Handley Page, flush with a £1,000 down payment from an impulsive German princess who was determined to make the flight, began designing a swept-wing cabin biplane with the Atlantic in mind.

Ill fortune intervened in the preparations of two other British contenders. A popular stunt pilot, Gustav Hamel, had announced brashly that he could make the flight in 16 hours. He ordered from the Martin and Handasyde company a huge, 215-horsepower wing-warping monoplane equipped with a watertight hull and discardable wheels. But on May 23, 1914, while flying a Morane-Saulnier monoplane over the English Channel, Hamel vanished without a trace, and his Atlantic-prize plane was never completed. Samuel Cody, another contender, had paid a French firm $3,000 to begin work on a 400-horsepower, 12-cylinder engine for a projected float monoplane, a monster in the Cody tradition, with a 120-foot wingspread, a top speed of 90 miles per hour, a fuel capacity of one and a half tons and places for a crew of three. But Cody too was killed—ironically while testing a smaller machine he had built for a seaplane race sponsored by Lord Northcliffe as a warm-up to the great transatlantic contest.

In February 1914, news filtered out of Glenn Curtiss' headquarters at Hammondsport, New York, that he too was preparing to take up Lord Northcliffe's challenge. Curtiss had been working quietly on a flying boat that he intended to have flown across the Atlantic by a two-man Anglo-American crew in celebration of the century of peace that had existed between Britain and the United States since the War of 1812.

The Philadelphia department-store scion, Rodman Wanamaker, who was financing Curtiss' project, declared that "it would be a fitting climax of the celebration if the two countries could link themselves by this international flight, demonstrating to the world that the time for disarmament of the nations is at hand, if for no other reason than because aeronautics has reached a stage where even the greatest dreadnought battleships may become futile in their power." Though Wanamaker was wrong about disarmament and premature in his assessment of air power, his money made possible the building of not one but two magnificent machines.

Christened *America,* the Curtiss flying boat was the largest airplane yet built in the United States. It was a pusher biplane with twin 100-horsepower engines, a 74-foot upper wing and a 30-foot hull framed with ash and spruce and planked with cedar. Atop the hull sat a spacious enclosed cockpit with celluloid windows and room inside for a navigating table and a mattress that doubled as a life raft. As a backup, a duplicate of the *America* was constructed.

While combing the United States Navy for an American copilot, Curtiss and Wanamaker selected a former British Royal Navy lieutenant, John Cyril Porte, as chief pilot of the *America*. Porte had first flown in a Demoiselle in 1910 and then graduated to Deperdussins. Invalided from the Navy with tuberculosis, he had become the London agent for Deperdussin; the British aviation press judged him a "superlative" flier.

Porte arrived in New York in late February 1914 in the middle of renewed fighting between those old antagonists, Glenn Curtiss and Orville Wright. The Wright Company had just won its patent suit against Curtiss, and Orville now threatened to stop the Atlantic flight unless Curtiss paid him royalties—not that Orville considered the Curtiss flying boat capable of making the trip. "I know that the machine cannot and will not cross the Atlantic," Orville snorted. The bickering was more than Porte had bargained for. While Orville and Curtiss continued to trade accusations, Porte took the train for Hammondsport, muttering to reporters, "Oh Lord, let me out of this; it's going to be a nasty mess."

Complications of a different sort awaited him at Hammondsport's Keuka Lake. Trials of the *America* began smoothly enough. On a test run on June 27, the plane flew two miles with seven men on board. Two days later, with eight newsmen on board, Porte got the craft up for a hop of 100 feet. "Steady as a bloomin' rock," he said confidently. But as the tests continued, a problem of lift developed. Carrying a ton of ballast that simulated its prospective fuel load, the *America* would not "unstick" from the water.

Preparations for an imminent Atlantic crossing continued nevertheless. Steamer reservations were made for Newfoundland, the projected takeoff point. Fuel was stockpiled in the Azores, where Porte intended to refuel. Bilingual notices in English and Portuguese went out to ships' masters, asking them to be on the lookout for the *America,* graphically described—for the benefit of old salts unfamiliar with this new craft—as "an aeroplane with boat attached, painted red."

In Hammondsport, meanwhile, Curtiss engineers fiddled with the flying boat's hull. Pontoons were added and discarded, a new hull configuration was tried and abandoned; finally a third engine was mounted above the cabin to provide more lift on takeoff and for use in emergencies. The *America* could now escape the water surface with a 2,600-pound load, and Curtiss professed delight: "I want more ballast," he exulted. "I can't hold her down."

But the third propeller, a tractor between the two pushers, tended to windmill in flight, creating excessive drag. That problem had just about been solved when, in August 1914, war began in Europe. All plans for transatlantic flight were set aside for the duration. Fittingly, it would be a Curtiss flying boat that would be first to cross the Atlantic in 1919.

The *America* and its twin, conceived to celebrate peace and promote disarmament, ironically were soon involved in the Great War. Sold to Britain over the protests of the German ambassador to Washington, the two flying boats were shipped to England in September 1914. The *America* was assigned to antisubmarine patrol, and at Lieutenant

The champagne christening of the Curtiss-built flying boat America in June 1914 drenches British pilot John C. Porte (right foreground). Porte had signed to fly the plane across the Atlantic, but the outbreak of war precluded the attempt.

Porte's urging, the British had Glenn Curtiss build them 50 more like it.

Aviation's first, and perhaps most colorful, decade was over. In the flick of time since the first flights at Kitty Hawk, man had established himself in the new element. By 1914, planes had been built that could climb to 20,000 feet, travel as fast as 127 miles per hour, cover 635 miles without a stop—and perhaps even cross the ocean. The roster of those who had mastered the rudiments of flying had grown from only two—Wilbur and Orville Wright—to more than 2,000 men and women who could call themselves aviators.

Such progress had not come without cost. Well over 200 people had lost their lives in accidents, prompting Anthony Fokker, even before the War began, to say that "every flying field I have ever known is soaked with the blood of my friends and brother pilots." For this brotherhood, however, the appeal of aviation remained irresistible. Exhibition pilot Ralph Johnstone, during his short lifetime, described what he called the intoxication of flying: "When you get in the air," he wrote, "the easy motion, the sense of freedom, the birdlike facility of flight—these qualities lead a man into a calmness that is almost hypnotic." It was a sensation that no earthbound experience could match. ᗌ

Exotic visitors to familiar sites

Through the earliest years of aviation, going up in an airplane was as chancy as a throw of the dice; the odds on a crash landing were all too great. As a result, most pilots stayed prudently away from populated areas. But as the aviators got better and their planes became safer, inhibitions relaxed; for the first time, city dwellers could enjoy the sight of an occasional flying machine swooping overhead without feeling they had better duck for cover.

Although the planes alone were attention getters, pilots soon added a classic touch to their aerial performances by flying against backdrops of famous landmarks. Celebrated structures in the world's great cities, from the Eiffel Tower in Paris to the White House in Washington, became pylons for races and end points for distance flights. The spectators and the photographers of the day found this combination of the familiar and the exotic hard to resist. Here and on the following pages are photographs of the first flights over, around or through five such landmarks.

The Count de Lambert flies around the Eiffel Tower in 1909. His Wright biplane cleared the top of the 984-foot-high tower by some 300 feet.

Inspired by a fictional aviator who circled the Tower of Pisa, Italy's Mario Cobianchi does it himself in 1911.

Umberto Cagno approaches St. Mark's in 1911 during the first flight over Venice. He landed on the Lido.

Frank McClean electrifies London by flying through the Tower Bridge in 1912. Soon afterward his plane crashed in the Thames but he survived.

Harry Atwood caps a record-breaking flight of 461 miles from Boston in 1911 by buzzing the White House before landing on the South Lawn.

Acknowledgments

The index for this book was prepared by Gale Linck Partoyan. The editors wish to thank John Amendola, artist *(pages 108-113, 148-149),* and Paul Lengellé, artist *(front endpaper and cover detail, regular edition).*

For their valuable help with the preparation of this volume, the editors wish to thank: **In France:** Châlons sur Marne—Georges Dumas, Directeur des Archives de la Marne; Le Mans—Henri Delgove; Paris—Gérard Baschet, Éditions de l'Illustration: Jacques Borgé; Pierre Breguet; Pierre Devambez; Isabelle Jammes; Jacques Lartigue; André Bénard, Odile Benoist, Elisabeth Caquot, Lucette Charpentier, Alain Degardin, Georges Delaleau, Gilbert Deloizy, Général Paul Dompnier, Deputy Director, Yvan Kayser, Général Pierre Lissarague, Director, Stephane Nicolaou, Colonel Jean-Baptiste Reveilhac, Curator, Musée de l'Air; Edmond Petit, Curator, Musée Air-France; Poissy—Jeanne Damamme, Curator, Musée du Jouet; Saint Romain-de-Colbosc—Claude-François Labarre. **In Italy:** Milan—Maurizio Pagliano, "Ali Italiane" Rizzoli; Sandro Taragni; Rome—Colonel Gennaro Adamo, Stato Maggiore Aeronautica; Countess Maria Fede Caproni, Museo Aeronautico Caproni di Taliedo. **In Japan:** Tokyo—Tadashi Nozawa. **In Switzer-** **land:** Lucerne—Verkehrsmuseum. **In the United States:** Connecticut—William Lee; Bea La-Flamme, Harvey Lippincott, United Technologies Archives; Washington, D.C.—William Leary, National Archives; Catherine D. Scott, Philip Edwards, Mary Pavlovich, Mimi Scharf, Karl P. Suthard, Robert van der Linden, National Air and Space Museum; Illinois—Archie Motley, Chicago Historical Society; Maryland—Lillian and William Gottschalk; Massachusetts—Mary Leen, Librarian, Thomas Parker, Director, The Bostonian Society; Winifred Collins, Massachusetts Historical Society; Larry Lewis; Martha Mahard, Harvard Theatre Collection; Mildred O'Connell, Museum of Transportation; Helen Slotkin, Massachusetts Institute of Technology; Michigan—Douglas Bakken, Joan Gartland, Cynthia Read, Henry Ford Museum; New Jersey—David Winans; New York—Owen Billman; Russell Crimi, New York Public Library; Davis Erhardt, Long Island Division, Queens Borough Public Library; Carl Hennicke; Eugene Husting; William Kaiser, Curator, Cradle of Aviation Museum; H. Schoenenberg, Grumman History Center; Richard Sherer; Merrill Stickler, Curator, Glenn H. Curtiss Museum; Ray Tillman; Ohio—Sid Bradd; Royal Frey, Curator, Charles Worman, Chief of Research, U.S. Air Force Museum; H. Eugene Kniess, National Cash Register Co.; Harold and Ivonette Wright Miller; Patrick Nolan, Wright State University Archives; George Page; Pennsylvania—David K. Bausch; Virginia—Dana Bell, U.S. Air Force Photo Depository; Washington—Peter Bowers. **In the Union of Soviet Socialist Republics:** Moscow—Museum of Aviation and Cosmonautics. **In West Germany:** Deisenhofen—Josef Pöllitsch; Munich—Herbert Studtrucker, Deutsches Museum; West Berlin—Roland Klemig, Heidi Klein, Bildarchiv Preussischer Kulturbesitz.

The editors also wish to thank Helen Cullinan, Cleveland; Rose-Mary Cason, Dallas; Diane Asselin, Los Angeles; Alison Raphael, Rio de Janeiro. Particularly useful sources of information and quotations used in this volume were: *The Rebirth of European Aviation 1902-1908: A Study of the Wright Brothers' Influence* by Charles H. Gibbs-Smith, Her Majesty's Stationery Office, London, 1974; *The First to Fly* by Sherwood Harris, Simon and Schuster, 1970; *Takeoff into Greatness: How American Aviation Grew so Big so Fast* by Grover Loening, G.P. Putnam's Sons, 1968; and *Miracle at Kitty Hawk: The Letters of Wilbur and Orville Wright,* Fred C. Kelly, ed., Farrar, Straus and Young, 1951.

Bibliography

Ajalbert, Jean, *La Passion de Roland Garros.* Paris: Les Éditions de France.

American Heritage, *History of Flight.* Simon & Schuster, 1962.

Angelucci, Enzo, and Paolo Matricardi, *World Aircraft: Origins—World War I.* Rand McNally, 1975.

Apostolo, Giorgio, *Color Profiles of World War I Combat Planes.* Crescent Books, 1973.

Beaumont, André, *My Three Big Flights.* London: Eveleigh Nash, 1912.

Blériot, Louis, and Edouard Ramond, *La Gloire Des Ailes: L'Aviation de Clement Ader A Costes.* Paris: Les Éditions de France.

Cahisa, Raymond, *L'Aviation D'Ader et des temps héroiques.* Paris: Éditions Albin Michel, 1950.

Collin, Ferdinand, *Parmi Les Précurseurs de Ciel.* Pevronnet & Cie.

Curtiss, Glenn H., and Augustus Post, *The Curtiss Aviation Book.* Frederick A. Stokes, 1912.

DeHavilland, Sir Geoffrey, *Sky Fever.* Shrewsbury: Airlife Publications, 1979.

De La Vaulx, Henry, *Le Triomphe de la Navigation Aérienne.* Paris: Librairie Illustrée, 1911.

Ferber, Andrée and Robert, *Les Débuts véritables de L'Aviation Française.* Fayard, 1970.

Fontaine, Charles, *Comment Blériot a Traverse la Manche.* Paris: Librairie Aéronautique, 1909.

Garros, Roland, *Mémoires.* Paris: Librairie Hachette, 1966.

Gastambide, Robert, *L'Envol.* Librairie Gallimard.

Gibbs-Smith, Charles H.:
Aviation: An Historical Survey from its Origins to the End of World War II. London: Her Majesty's Stationery Office, 1970.
Clément Ader: His Flight-Claims and his Place in History. London: Her Majesty's Stationery Office, 1968.
A Directory and Nomenclature of the First Aeroplanes: 1809 to 1909. London: Her Majesty's Stationery Office, 1966.
The Invention of the Aeroplane (1799-1909). Taplinger Publishing Co., 1965.
The Rebirth of European Aviation 1902-1908: A Study of the Wright Brothers' Influence. London: Her Majesty's Stationery Office, 1974.

Grahame-White, Claude, *The Story of the Aeroplane.* Small, Maynard and Company, 1911.

Harper, Harry, *Twenty-five Years of Flying: Impressions, Recollections, and Descriptions.* London: Hutchinson & Co.

Harris, Sherwood, *The First to Fly: Aviation's Pioneer Days.* Simon and Schuster, 1970.

Hatfield, D. D., *Dominguez Air Meet.* Northrop University Press, 1976.

Jane's Historical Aircraft 1902-1916. Doubleday, 1972.

Kelly, Fred C., *The Wright Brothers.* Ballantine Books, 1943.

Kelly, Fred C., ed., *Miracle at Kitty Hawk: The Letters of Wilbur and Orville Wright.* Farrar, Straus and Young, 1951.

Laignier, G. H., *Livre D'Or de la Grande Semaine d'Aviation de la Champagne.*

Lecerf, Pierre, and A. de Castillon de Saint-Victor, *Deux Héros de l'Air:Chavez et Bielovucic.* Paris: Nouvelles Éditions Latines.

Lee, Arthur Gould, *The Flying Cathedral.* London: Methuen & Co., 1965.

Lefevre, Georges, *Louis Blériot.* Paris: Librairie de "L'Auto," 1909.

Lhospice, Michel, *Match Pour La Manche.* Denoël, 1964.

Lieberg, Owen S., *The First Air Race: The International Competition at Reims, 1909.* Doubleday, 1974.

Loening, Grover:
Our Wings Grow Faster. Doubleday, Doran, 1935.
Takeoff into Greatness: How American Aviation Grew so Big so Fast. G. P. Putnam's Sons, 1968.

McFarland, Marvin W., ed., *The Papers of Wilbur and Orville Wright:*
Volume One: 1899-1905. Arno, 1972.
Volume Two: 1906-1948. Arno, 1972.

McMahon, John R., *The Wright Brothers: Fathers of Flight.* Little, Brown, 1930.

Macmillan, Norman, *Great Airmen.* London: G. Bell and Sons, 1955.

Maitland, Lester J., *Knights of the Air.* Doubleday, Doran, 1929.

Morris, Lloyd, and Kendall Smith, *Ceiling Unlimited: The Story of American Aviation from Kitty Hawk to Supersonics.* Macmillan, 1953.

Morrow, John Howard, Jr., *Building German Airpower, 1909-1914.* University of Tennessee Press, 1976.

Mortane, Jacques:
Les Ailes Glorieuses. Paris: Éditions Baudiniere, 1936.
Les Héros de L'Air. Paris: Librairie Delagrave, 1930.

Munson, Kenneth, *Pioneer Aircraft: 1903-1914.* Macmillan, 1969.

Nowarra, Heinz J., and G. R. Duval, *Russian Civil and Military Aircraft 1884-1969.* London: Fountain Press, 1971.

Parkin, J. H., *Bell and Baldwin: Their Development of Aerodromes and Hydrodromes at Baddeck, Nova Scotia.* University of Toronto Press, 1964.

Penrose, Harald, *British Aviation: The Pioneer Years 1903-1914.* London: Putnam, 1967.

Renstrom, Arthur G., *Wilbur & Orville Wright: A Chronology Commemorating the Hundredth Anniversary of the Birth of Orville Wright.* Library of Congress, 1975.

Roseberry, C. R., *Glenn Curtiss: Pioneer of Flight.*

Doubleday, 1972.

Sahel, Jacques, *Henry Farman et L'Aviation.* Grasset, 1936.

Sauvage, Roger, *Les Conquérants de Ciel.* Paris: Le Livre Artistique, 1960.

Scharff, Robert, and Walter S. Taylor, *Over Land and Sea: A Biography of Glenn Hammond Curtiss.* David McKay Company, 1968.

Studer, Clara, *Sky Storming Yankee: The Life of Glenn Curtiss.* Stackpole Sons, 1937.

Sunderman, James F., ed., *Early Air Pioneers*

1862-1935. Franklin Watts, 1961.

Turner, C. C., *The Old Flying Days.* Arno, 1972.

Villard, Henry Serrano, *Contact! The Story of the Early Birds.* Bonanza Books, 1968.

Voisin, Gabriel, *Men, Women and 10,000 Kites.* London: Putnam, 1963.

Walker, Percy B., *Early Aviation at Farnborough: The History of the Royal Aircraft Establishment: Volume One: Balloons, Kites and Airships.* London: Macdonald, 1971.

Volume Two: The First Aeroplanes. London:

Macdonald, 1974.

Wallace, Graham:
  Claude Grahame-White: A Biography. London: Putnam, 1960.
  Flying Witness: Harry Harper and the Golden Age of Aviation. London: Putnam, 1958.

Wykeham, Peter, *Santos-Dumont: A Study in Obsession.* London: Putnam, 1962.

Periodicals

Dollfus, Charles, *Icare,* No. 64, 1973.

Picture credits

Index

Printed in U.S.A.